THE ART OF LIVING WITHOUT TENSION

Previous Books by David Seabury

HIGH HOPES FOR LOW SPIRITS

HOW JESUS HEALS OUR MINDS TODAY

HELP YOURSELF TO HAPPINESS

THE ART OF SELFISHNESS

UNMASKING OUR MINDS

GROWING INTO LIFE

WHAT MAKES US SEEM SO QUEER

KEEP YOUR WITS

HOW TO WORRY SUCCESSFULLY

BUILD YOUR OWN FUTURE

HOW TO GET THINGS DONE

ADVENTURES IN SELF-DISCOVERY

SEE YOURSELF AS OTHERS SEE YOU

WHY WE LOVE AND HATE

THE ART OF LIVING
Without Tension

By David Seabury

HARPER & BROTHERS · PUBLISHERS · NEW YORK

Distributed by
DE VORSS & CO.
516 W. NINTH STREET
LOS ANGELES 15, CALIF.

To all those Presidents of the United States who have given to us their lives because of the strain of overwork,

To those living men of medicine and science whose days are full of stress because of the intensity of their toil,

To all those men of business whose years are being shortened by lack of knowing how to work without tension,

To all the mothers and saintly women whose days are full of weariness because of faithful striving, this book is gratefully dedicated. May its pages bring them comfort, rest and a blessed easing of their strain.

TABLE OF CONTENTS

THE ART OF LIVING WITHOUT TENSION

THE QUESTION OF ADVICE

*A*T ONE time or another strain visits each of us. It troubles our days and gives us restless nights. You remember, do you not, occasions when you could not sleep? You may have stood at your window looking into the sky. Long thoughts flooded your mind: questions that search the farthest stars.

What is life all about? How can happiness be found? Why are some people lucky, others unfortunate? Who can tell you what to do in love and in life?

You may now have no time or inclination to look at the stars, but do you not still wonder how life can be richer, more comfortable and joyous, not so full of exhaustion and uncertainty?

Many years ago, when my own questioning began, I sat on

the knee of William James while he talked over problems of adjustment with my father. "Why is it people make life so difficult?" he would ask. Then they were off in a discussion that included the teachings of Lao-tse, Plato and the history of thought, until a little boy's head went around and around.

Nevertheless, in the decades that followed, William James taught me how to live without tension. He told me to "listen to my mind" so that I would guide my doing more thoughtfully. He explained how to avoid nervous concern with the consequences of effort. He showed me how to relax when the demon of duty got me in his grip. Again and again he spoke of a "second wind" that would come to sustain me if I persisted quietly.

During the years as a consulting psychologist I have tried to use this information helpfully. It had saved me so much strain I longed to have others share my benefit. At the same time, the problem arose as to the wisdom of telling others how they should endeavor to live. One of the greatest of our modern techniques is to help people to discover for themselves what to do and how to do it. This procedure is called the non-directive method. Its value is unquestionable.

At the same time, many are they among leaders in clinical work who believe that adjustment psychology is quite as important as any of the analytic procedures. They feel that many of the therapies need explaining and would not easily be acquired by people without assistance. There is no question that this was the attitude of William James. Because, however, it is startlingly easy to assume an authoritarian position, even without realizing one has done so, I have endeavored where possible never to give advice. I have faith in the non-directive procedures. I believe in helping people to think out their own solutions. Such a method, however, requires much time and more space. To present the means

2

for easing out of strain that are in this book, in the "let's think it out together" manner, would necessitate a text of half a million words.

After years of listening to the problems of people, I am surely entitled to say, "My clinical experience has taught me this," and, "After a lifetime of thinking about it, I've come to the conclusion you will be happier and healthier if . . ."

Frankly, this book does give advice. In it are techniques that can protect you from much sorrow. At the same time, you will find no rosy promise that your life will be a gay, sweet song, unless you learn to make it so. Life is life, and life is difficult. It requires wise handling. Few of us believe the vapid affirmations some people utter. Bland optimism is as dangerous, and as far off balance, as negativity. Neither attitude is sane.

"Man," wrote Disraeli, "is not a creature of circumstance, but circumstances are creatures of man." That, in a single sentence, is the philosophy of this book.

A careful study of biography, whatever else it shows, reveals beyond question that men and women of great achievement never gave up their determination to overcome the odds against them. They planned and organized their way to wealth, fame or exceptional service. Differing as to their purposes, the persistency of their desires seems to have been one and the same.

To follow their example and thus achieve success, what must we do? If we pause long enough in our social onrush to think about it, the answer becomes clear. Since the stress of circumstance is received within ourselves the solution starts within ourselves. It requires that we see and organize our desires, that we plan a way of life suited to our special natures. Who are you? Who am I? Where are we going in such a hurry?

When we arrive we must act, must we not, from ourselves and be ourselves? We cannot otherwise adjust to so intensified a world. We cannot successfully do what we must do, know how to do it, or why it must be done, if we cannot muster our make-up and assemble our sanity for the tasks that come upon us. There is no power within us if we hear only the echoes that bounce against the wall of ancient prejudice.

Success is, of course, a matter of personal adaptation to the ever changing environment of modern life. Release from stress is achieved by the simple yet profoundly important method of designing your thought in advance of effort, by a union of visual imagery, autosuggestion and persistent application. These three great means of self-direction, when used until they become unconscious habits, can and will reshape your life as completely as science and engineering have transformed your material environment.

To help us to see more clearly how adjustment is achieved let us reduce the basis of everyone's experience to six short phrases:

I AM

I WANT

I HAVE

I CAN

I MAY

I MUST

Any and all adjustment begins with you, and depends upon what you are. If you were not, no problem would exist, for you at least. It comes into being because you are. It is measured and shaped by what you are. For you, the "I am" is the major issue, whatever the world about you becomes.

As soon as you were born, however, you began to want,

4

even if it was limited to finding your mother's breasts. As you grew, your wants increased until they seemed to become greater than the who and what you are. Yet the "I am" still determined the nature of the "I want" and designated how you secured it from your environment.

After a while this wanting gave you possessions: a sense of what you had and what you did not have. What you *had* became a problem, the thought of what you did *not* have a nervous fret.

Keenly aware of the resultant feeling of insecurity, your lacks made you consult with yourself as to how you could gain more of your wants. In doing this, you discovered the limits of your power to achieve. "I can" then became your center of anticipation: a measure in your mind of the strength of the "I am."

After a while you discovered that your "I can" did not always accomplish your purpose to have more. There were others about you whose "wants" and "cans" sought to gain the same ends. In the struggle that ensued conflict developed.

Society then stepped in to restrict you both. Thus your "I can" turned into an "I may," and into an "I may not" wherever restraint, wise or otherwise, had been established.

So it was that your "I must" came into being: what you must do to win your way with available opportunity and against those restrictions that spring from man's ignorance of how to live. You also found, to your chagrin, that, to survive, your adjustment was even more a question of what you must *not* do. Here is where pain entered. You may have been taught to accept limitation that could destroy your life, unwisely delimit your success, obliterate your happiness, causing you years of misfortune.

As you reached maturity, it was for you to decide (if you could) how you would live. The question is still before you.

5

Will you remain a slave to the ways of strain no matter how destructive, or will you set yourself free by the use of methods suited to a mechanical age?

To find the answer, you must again realize your "I am," and because of who you are make your choice. You will be helped to this decision by seeing how antiquated ways and abnormal beliefs make people fail. You discover that such setness and compromise do not in the end accomplish the purpose they were expected to perform. Nature refuses to be cheated.

Nor is it nature only you must obey, for nature is but an attribute of the universe in which are principles whose powers are inviolate. Through knowing of cosmic order science came into being. Because of it, engineering was made possible. From obedience to it came the conquest of the earth.

Our environment, then, is more than natural. It is also a world of man-made machines, which, however, were produced by fulfilling natural law. We realize that our surroundings have been transformed by the work of chemists and physicists. We must remind ourselves that the means by which this miracle was achieved must also be obeyed in our personal lives. In other words, organized methods must be used in handling our experience. There is otherwise no way out of trouble. There was, and also is, no other way for mankind. It can, if it will, avoid the doom that otherwise looms ahead. Man can by facing forward bring forth a new age.

He will do this, however, only by a wise use of the practical techniques that have been developed in this century. Few would deny that the industrial period which has so eased our bodily pressures came into being from scientific research. The psychological age we are now entering is coming from an equally sound approach. It will bring to you, if you let it, an even greater release from discomfort and fatigue. It will

6

give you a deeper joy than anything chemistry and mechanics have achieved. They have eased the life of your body. It is you and your mind which need the solace that is at hand.

In this book are twenty-four steps in the art of living without tension. Each of them is helpful but by itself is not enough.

The life we live is so complex in such a world as ours, we must have at our command means that are adequate to deal with the complexity. Thus we must not only learn how to use each method, but how to create a union of them into one great therapy.

When this merging is achieved we then have in our possession a means for the control of strain and for the accomplishment of our desires that functions spontaneously and without conscious effort. It carries you through life. You do not have to carry it.

1 OUR UNBALANCED WORLD

*P*ERSONAL experience is more intimately real than anything in life. As we rise in the morning, it closes about us as possessively as a penurious relative. Bright or dark, gay or sad, it becomes our part of this tumultuous world.

Consider your own drama. Have you not sat long hours, trying to fight through the problems that mount so mercilessly? Have you not brooded on the routine of it all: work, sleep, work, sleep, on and on like the tramp of marching men?

Such strains are not more common, however, than the problem of keeping your earning power, while you wonder how you can endure the tyranny of your daughter's tears. Like ubiquitous insects, the nig-nags come: trouble with your neighbors, and the antics of children. If you do not feel like a marionette with some force beyond you pulling the strings, you are an exceptional person.

9

Independence is our national watchword, but independence from what? Such experience? Can you claim it? Is your life without pressure, in the home or at your work? When and where are you free?

It is the tenet of modern psychology that you have a right to live without coercion: we believe that being comes before doing; that all doing should be determined by the nature of one's being. This is freedom indeed. It is good theory. It ought to be good practice. It can be, if we know how to use the right means.

Whatever our future, we have only the present to live in. Without new insight, the affect of our past upon the present may well nigh engulf us.

Successfully to solve the problems of a colonial farm was not difficult. The needs and obstacles repeated themselves. That they called for heroism, none will deny. It was, however, a natural heroism produced by the act of conquering the land.

If you had wished to travel from the Atlantic to the Pacific two hundred years ago, you would have depended upon the skills and strength of your body. Going most of the way on foot, only your wits and muscles could have seen you through. In this modern life you now use an instrument, a fast plane perhaps, covering the distance in a day that would have required months of hardship. Must you not now also have mental processes that are equally swift?

Had you at that time wished to send a message to a loved one miles away, it would have been carried on foot, on horseback or by the uncertainties of a sailing vessel. Now you use air mail, telegraph or call long distance. You meet your material problems by modern means. Success requires that you meet your mental problems by equally new ways.

When a stick was only a stick and a stone only a stone, there was no need to discover subjective ways to avoid failure. Reality was limited to the use of one's senses. People placed little value on the opinions of an idealist who talked about the forces of life that must be considered to keep life in balance. They did not foresee that mechanical progress might sweep ahead, leaving our knowledge of the art of living no better than it was centuries ago. They had little use for values that could not be placed in nicely set categories. Practicality consisted in how to make people and substances obey one's will. To average men anything beyond physical manifestations was of no importance. Real estate, the clearing of land, the planting of crops, the harvesting of grains, the catching of fish, the raising and butchering of animals were the major activities.

Nowadays we talk of light waves that take millions of years to reach us and of rocket ships to the moon. Billions of our tax money are spent to create bombs, based upon elements no one's eyes have ever seen. Young men spend lonely years manning warning stations somewhere near the North Pole. Others fly on interminable missions out to sea. Electric eyes open and close all sorts of contraptions. Robots do the work that once required hordes of men.

The world of activity is changed and constantly changing. Yet do you believe the average man's idea of what is practical to think, to feel and to do in his own life has matured to meet this era of invisible power? He may assume he is modern in his ideas, and maybe he is. It is possible. Is it equally probable?

As a consulting psychologist I have talked with countless people only to discover the almost shocking truth that they have become sophisticated intellectually as to radio, radar, electronics and the general picture of an atomic age, but follow ideas of long passed centuries in the way they operate their lives. Few, if any of them, took time to use constructive methods to fulfill their purposes or even knew that such methods exist.

When one has lost his reason we speak of him in common parlance as unbalanced. Is not a man unbalanced who endeavors to live in an airplane world with a horse and buggy philosophy? Has he not abandoned his intelligence when he strives to solve his personal difficulties by the mere use of his wits, and without a constructive means that helps his wits to work efficiently? In an age when man lived only by the toil of his hands, to depend upon his own ego was in all ways consistent. To assume that his personal attributes, when left unorganized, are of themselves adequate for the speeds and complexities of a mechanical world is insane. Here lies the tragedy and the cause of our ever increasing number of mental breakdowns.

The solution of this dilemma is clear. We must have at our command a score of thinking methods suitable to our day and age. We must acquire means of achievement that are as advanced over those of the hand-weaving centuries as is a modern factory run by automation. The processes by which we endeavor to meet the problems of our day must fit its conditions. To the degree that these problems differ from those of the past, so must the methods we use to deal with them. That is the stark truth. He who does not listen to and obey it is doomed to failure in love, life and the pursuit of happiness.

Let us not become machines. Let us use them. Let us learn from the inventions that have so changed our physical world how to create ways to run our mental machinery with ease. That is the modern spirit. We shall not solve our problems by reverting to the old ways or denying the new ones.

When I am asked to give advice to those still immersed in the old turmoils, I start with a few simple words. If listened to and applied, they lay a sure foundation for living without strain. I have found, however, that I have to repeat those few words over and over again to gain a true response.

I say to people, "When you have a problem to solve, don't

do it yourself; find some method or instrument to work for you." Simple advice, you say. Most people ignore it, however. They strive as if they must grapple all experience with their bare hands. They live their intimate lives depending upon their own personal power.

Millions who use tools, machines and innumerable gadgets to accomplish their physical tasks never stop to find equivalent mental means to achieve their personal desires. In consequence, instead of living orderly lives they struggle in a helter-skelter experience. We who see them wearing themselves out cry, "Stop—stop this blind, self-involved struggle. Stop to observe the sort of world you live in. Stop to see that there are easier ways of doing what you do than existed in 1958 B.C."

Even in those days there were some instruments, such as the wheel, already discovered, on which a person could have patterned his thought and from which he could have created easier ways of conduct. Take the case of Conrad Almsworth. To see him wearing himself out with the responsibilities of his home and office, one might suppose him to be psychically blind. He approaches every task as if only by personal effort could it be accomplished. Tension grips him during his business hours. Responsibility is a heavy burden. He pushes at his problems in exactly the spirit a primitive man had to use to lift a stone before he discovered the efficiency of a lever. Nor is it only in his business hours that this undue effort controls Conrad. The behavior of his children, and even his wife's nonchalant manner, are a constant worry. He believes they should follow his strenuous example; that otherwise they will become as irresponsible and self-indulgent as the shiftless millions he sees about him.

In this reference, there are today three sorts of people in the world: first, those who toil with the same slavery to personal effort that men were forced to use centuries ago; second, those who leave tasks unfinished or poorly done, because of indifference. They are the rebellious people with no sense of responsibility or good workmanship, people who believe in "getting by" if they can. As children they became disobedient and pleasure seeking as a result of the coercion toward personal effort put upon them by adults. Disillusioned as to the worth of toil, they lost the ethical sense of honest achievement.

Neither the group who live by the "get the money any way you can" spirit, nor yet the followers of Conrad Almsworth's slavery are apt to be successful. Both of these groups live haphazard lives, unaware that there are easy and efficient ways by which they may think their way into practical and successful achievement. The third group of men and women are few in number compared to those who painfully toil and those who irresponsibly cheat. They are the people who stop to design the ways by which easy and successful accomplishment is brought to pass. You will admit this is by far the smallest in number of the three kinds of people. Their ideas have form and structure, even as the instruments, tools and machines they use in this modern world of mechanics have form and structure. You would call a farmer a fool who tried to move a boulder with his two hands and did not stop to get a crowbar. Are we not somewhat foolish if we neglect to use the instruments of mental efficiency that are now available?

In so complex a social order, with such varied tasks in it, nothing can be done well unless such modern methods are used. People vaguely know this fact, but fail to apply it in practical ways. Yet the principle is before them. No builder would think of going to work on the construction of a house unless he possessed an architectural plan to direct his effort. No maker of machinery starts to produce an engine until the mechanical drawing is completed. Nor does this mean a mere picture of the whole instrument. It means the drafting of each part with a clear knowledge of how each element fits with each other element to fulfill its use. The whole machine is a union of those parts conceived on the basis of how they are to co-operate.

This principle of design is the basis of all the great instruments we have in our modern civilization. When it is understood and used in one's personal life strain and pressure abate and the prevalent confusion departs. This truth should be apparent to everyone. It is evident in such activities as building houses or making machines. Yet even with supposedly good blueprints many houses are built without solid construction, adequate closets, sound ventilation and correct lighting. If this can be so, think what a mess many a house would be if it were erected with no plans at all. As for machines, they could not even be conceived unless an inventor had a clear picture in his mind of how the instrument was to work and its parts be put together for an ultimate use.

Every successful aspect of achievement in modern life obeys this principle of design. Even the making of a good bowl of soup needs a recipe, and as for bringing up a baby no educated mother would neglect to follow efficient methods. She knows that only from obedience to definite steps and precise formulas is infant mortality no longer a tragic commonplace.

Strangely enough it seldom occurs to such a mother that just as concise arrangements are essential to the happy and healthy living of her own personal life. Nor is this only true of how she uses her mind. It is just as true of how she expresses her emotions, and even more so as to how she treats her husband. And he, poor fellow, often exhibits the same strange neglect of adequate planning in his own life. He may possess all sorts of efficiency equipment in office, manufacturing plant and salesroom, and fail quite as completely as his wife to follow the principles of design in his more personal mental and emotional procedures.

Professor Oxon teaches in one of our great universities. His subject is physics, including research for the advancement of atomic energy. His mind is supposed to be trained to the most accurate forms of thought. But is this actually the case? If so, Professor Oxon would also live his personal life with care and forethought. He doesn't. It is as if he leaves his wits in his laboratory and returns to his home in the guise of a dormoron. One cannot, of course, call him a moron for he is a brilliant man of science. But his intelligence seems to blur as soon as he looks at his wife. And she, poor dear, cannot understand why he becomes as emotional as an adolescent girl when something goes wrong in their personal relations. "Men," she tells her close woman friend, "seem to be so stupid about the home, and especially in the handling of children. I am sure my husband wants to be a good father, but he is utterly inconsistent in the way he treats our boys."

It has apparently never occurred to Professor Oxon that if he were as inefficient in his laboratory as he is in his home he and many others would die.

Years ago a man came to me for help in his marriage. He was a successful executive, the head of a large firm. He directed his business with skill. His office ran smoothly and well. The rest of his life was chaos. I got him to face the fact that if he conducted his personal life as thoughtfully as he did his executive activities his experience would become transformed. I proved to him that he knew how to do it or he could not organize and direct his business activities as efficiently as he did. Accepting my analysis of his situation, he applied my conclusions with extraordinary results. He simply

16

had never thought of carrying out into his personal relations the attitudes and ways of living that have long been customary in science, engineering and industry.

To realize that we each and all of us can, if we will, cease to live helter-skelter lives is the first step in the conquest of strain.

2 ESTIMATING YOUR WAY OF LIFE

*I*N THE matter of advising people how to live in this unbalanced world there has been a most serious mistake made in recent years. Doctors, psychiatrists, psychologists, educators, all who are concerned with a person's mental health, have noted a tendency in us to retreat into pleasure seeking, shiftlessness and neurosis in order to escape from the hurly-burly and confusion of these transitory times. They have therefore advised us to "get back to reality."

Nothing more excellent could have been said had the rest of what needed to be said followed such an admonition. Few of these advisers seem to have explained *how* one was to "get back to reality" safely and successfully. This deficiency resulted in sending people back to physical activity without adequate preparation.

There are not many among us who listen well enough to what is said in an incomplete way to re-form, or rephrase, any such advice and thus to make it complete. As a result, "back to reality" was taken to mean go out physically and get into the world. Don't stop to see what the world is like, just go out into it.

The social order at the present time is in no sense a natural or normal state of being. It is a mixed-up turmoil because of the amazing advancement of mechanics and the tragic lack of knowledge as to how human nature should be handled. The fact that a person must first become adjusted to nature before he can successfully adjust to social custom has been sadly neglected. As a result, millions have applied the admonition "get back to reality" to mean go out into the helter-skelter, rushing life and depend on luck. Go to work. Get money if you can. But, in any case, jump into things. That is the impression that many have formed.

Because of this thoughtless misunderstanding of "get back to reality," the well-intended admonition of the world's counselors has played its part in the making of mental breakdowns. The *how* we should get back to reality should first have been explained. That this meant the use of what to many seemed to be part of the unreality added to the confusion. Wishful thinking, daydreams about one's longings and desires, hopeful plans for an as yet unreal tomorrow, ways of doing not unlike the contraptions in an inventor's mind; these all seemed to belong to the world of fantasy that people were advised to leave.

Few have been taught that there was meaning in their dreaming but that one must turn his imaginary thinking into concrete plans and definite conduct patterns designed to create a wise adjustment. Most people did not understand that creating a thoughtful pattern in one's mind of how one was to direct and control his relation to the world about him was equally a part of reality, and a most essential step in getting back to it.

19

If a chemical engineer, advised to "get back to reality," took it to mean that he should jump into material activity without a guiding pattern to direct his conduct, he would soon be blown to bits. Many are they who have nearly blown their wits to bits by jumping into the hurly-burly of materialism in a haphazard manner. Some have had insight and training enough in a special vocation to keep their heads at the daily task, only to lose it when leaving office, store or factory. Few indeed have understood the full art of living and thus have realized that in an unbalanced world personal balance within one's self must be achieved before one can safely go into action, and that one is lost without such an equilibrium.

Personal balance means that one has studied and learned to use ways of life, and methods of carefully directed conduct, that are suited to the state of the world in which he lives. Personal balance means that he does not rush into the hurly-burly in a helter-skelter manner, but directs his efforts wisely and calmly. It means that he uses forethought and planning much as a businessman organizes the activities of his commercial or industrial undertakings. But this has not been the way of most people in the doings of their personal lives. Nor is it typical of the general tenor of home and street.

When the rush hour comes morning and evening, how many poised and careful drivers do you see on our highways? How free is the traffic from egotistical competition and emotionalism? Great is the knowledge and great are the skills that produced the instruments we now possess. But we are still like children playing with explosives.

Sociologists and many other thoughtful people have asked, "What is the cause of worry and strain? Why are our hospital beds occupied with more mental cases than from any other cause? Why are there so many divorces and so much juvenile delinquency?"

The answer is clear. We have not been taught to direct our human relations with the same care that has created and transformed our material world. Many an aviator is skilled in the intricate art of blind flying, who has little knowledge and less training as to how to pass through the blinding fogs of marriage and parenthood. Many an adept in higher mathematics does not ever use the spirit of simple arithmetic when it comes to calculating what to do in his emotional experiences. Nor has anyone ever taught him how to add and subtract, multiply or divide, when he has to discover the facts of his personal problems. He goes at them as clumsily as primitive man counted out his values by piling up pebbles.

If in your own experience this helter-skelterness is apparent and you see it and face it, you have then put your finger on the cause of much of your unhappiness and strain.

Had mankind not discovered on the physical plane that this mass thoughtlessness was at the bottom of its toil and trouble, civilization would never have come to pass. Nor would we now possess the amazing instruments—our railroads and steamships, our airplanes and telephones—and all the other conveniences that ease our physical lives. Centuries ago, out of the turbid tribes, came a man here and there who looked beyond the tumult of his days and pondered as to how his physical life could be bettered, protected and organized. As his effort joined with that of other thinkers new ways of doing appeared.

As you and I in this still tumultuous world follow the example of these early men, and apply it to the command of our personal behavior, we bring to pass an equally great transformation. In so doing we change the current of our destiny.

It was from seeing the obstacles and needs that rose persistently before them that thoughtful men considered what to do. Seeking to deal with these requirements, they created the foundations of modern science, engineering, medicine, education and all that is constructive in civilization.

From seeing the obstacles and needs in your own life and by seeking to deal with their requirements, you create the foundations of personal happiness, success and security. Could any truth be simpler? Yet the helter-skelter basis still rules the ways of most people. Few control the current of events by thoughtful planning.

Psychoneurosis and insanity are almost unknown among primitive people, and most of them live far happier lives than we who call ourselves civilized. Must we not also admit that the art of living was as well understood centuries ago as it is now? Have we a culture equivalent to that of ancient Greece?

Here then is the central cause of trouble in your life and mine: our experience is unbalanced. We have knowledge and equipment with which to deal with the physical side of life. We lack, or do not use, knowledge and equipment on the personal, that is, the mental, emotional and spiritual, aspect of experience.

To correct this woeful deficiency there is obviously just one thing we should do: namely, to survey our personal setup in exactly the way men of science and engineering analyze the situations and materials that made possible the conquering of the physical world. They saw that needs and obstacles must be analyzed so that the right plans might be made and the necessary equipment secured. They studied the laws and principles of nature that must be clarified and obeyed. They used efficient ways of simplifying their tasks, adding, subtracting, multiplying and dividing the structures and facts with which they had to deal. Thus were their purposes organized.

Only as we follow their example, using the techniques that are now increasingly available, can we safely accept that most worth-while advice to "get back to reality." We must get back to it prepared to deal successfully with its problems. We must get back to it by means that are as efficient as those we use in our physical activities. Otherwise, the tension that results may destroy us.

There is no better way to learn what one's relation to reality is than frankly and fully to face oneself and one's way of life. It is easy to blame the world for the pressure and confusion under which we live. It is still easier to rationalize our failure to square up to the causes of tension. The following questionnaire, if carefully evaluated, has proved to be a turning point for many a person who had supposed that he was "doing all he could" in the various situations in which he found himself. Maybe he was "doing all he could" after he had let his troubles come upon him. Most of us are forced to make great effort when we are submerged by the circumstances for which we are unprepared. We seldom like to admit that most of our failures spring from a lack of organization.

The questionnaire is for the purpose of clarifying your own pattern of thought and activity, so as to suggest where sincere effort will bring about the most needed results. Few of us take time to scout out our strengths and weaknesses for the purpose of obtaining an effective balance in our life planning and thus eliminating waste of effort.

Evaluate this approximation as thoughtfully as you can. It requires contemplation and unsparing honesty. How much of what you do is carefully planned and part of a life program? Is your behavior directed to some degree by as wise a campaign as a general must use in determining the strategy which guides his army? Or do you have to deal with event after event that just seems to happen? Mark the test from zero to ten according to the amount of the factor involved.

DO YOU:

1. Jump to conclusions   0 1 2 3 4 5 6 7 8 9 10
2. Assume without assurances   0 1 2 3 4 5 6 7 8 9 10
3. Let first impressions rule you   0 1 2 3 4 5 6 7 8 9 10
4. Feel always under pressure   0 1 2 3 4 5 6 7 8 9 10
5. Let work pile up   0 1 2 3 4 5 6 7 8 9 10
6. Live in confusion   0 1 2 3 4 5 6 7 8 9 10
7. Become over-worked   0 1 2 3 4 5 6 7 8 9 10
8. Get in lots of messes   0 1 2 3 4 5 6 7 8 9 10
9. Suffer restlessness   0 1 2 3 4 5 6 7 8 9 10
10. Lack incentive   0 1 2 3 4 5 6 7 8 9 10
11. Often reconsider   0 1 2 3 4 5 6 7 8 9 10
12. Resent difficulties   0 1 2 3 4 5 6 7 8 9 10
13. Put things off   0 1 2 3 4 5 6 7 8 9 10
14. Make effort at random   0 1 2 3 4 5 6 7 8 9 10
15. Proceed without planning   0 1 2 3 4 5 6 7 8 9 10
16. Fail to evaluate carefully   0 1 2 3 4 5 6 7 8 9 10
17. Become over-involved in situations   0 1 2 3 4 5 6 7 8 9 10
18. Become nervous easily   0 1 2 3 4 5 6 7 8 9 10
19. Become scattered in your thinking   0 1 2 3 4 5 6 7 8 9 10
20. Often feel imposed on   0 1 2 3 4 5 6 7 8 9 10
21. Feel you do not have a fair chance   0 1 2 3 4 5 6 7 8 9 10

24

22.	Feel you are not appreciated	0	1	2	3	4	5	6	7	8	9	10
23.	Concentrate on negatives	0	1	2	3	4	5	6	7	8	9	10
24.	Sink into routine	0	1	2	3	4	5	6	7	8	9	10
25.	Let your thoughts ramble	0	1	2	3	4	5	6	7	8	9	10
26.	Depend on circumstances	0	1	2	3	4	5	6	7	8	9	10
27.	Feel you must compromise	0	1	2	3	4	5	6	7	8	9	10
28.	Feel you have to struggle	0	1	2	3	4	5	6	7	8	9	10
29.	Use guesswork for important things	0	1	2	3	4	5	6	7	8	9	10
30.	Use makeshifts	0	1	2	3	4	5	6	7	8	9	10
31.	Accept coercion	0	1	2	3	4	5	6	7	8	9	10
32.	Feel constantly irritated	0	1	2	3	4	5	6	7	8	9	10
33.	Let things get in a heap	0	1	2	3	4	5	6	7	8	9	10
34.	Expect to tolerate anything	0	1	2	3	4	5	6	7	8	9	10
35.	Let your attention wander	0	1	2	3	4	5	6	7	8	9	10
36.	Seldom feel relaxed											
37.	Feel you don't understand life	0	1	2	3	4	5	6	7	8	9	10
38.	Think of life as a struggle	0	1	2	3	4	5	6	7	8	9	10
39.	Sleep rather poorly	0	1	2	3	4	5	6	7	8	9	10
40.	Often use substitutes	0	1	2	3	4	5	6	7	8	9	10
41.	Become lost in effects	0	1	2	3	4	5	6	7	8	9	10
42.	Often have to forego things	0	1	2	3	4	5	6	7	8	9	10
43.	Live by chance	0	1	2	3	4	5	6	7	8	9	10

44.	Feel resigned	0 1 2 3 4 5 6 7 8 9 10
45.	Make haphazard choices	0 1 2 3 4 5 6 7 8 9 10
46.	Experience much disorder	0 1 2 3 4 5 6 7 8 9 10
47.	Experience much delay	0 1 2 3 4 5 6 7 8 9 10
48.	Depend on luck	0 1 2 3 4 5 6 7 8 9 10
49.	Often feel frustrated	0 1 2 3 4 5 6 7 8 9 10
50.	Feel all tired out	0 1 2 3 4 5 6 7 8 9 10

The highest possible negative score is 500. This can only be made by one whose life is in utter confusion. A score of 400 means that the person lets life come upon him with little forethought. A score of 300 still shows lack of preparation. If you can honestly achieve a score of only 200 you are already a convert to careful planning. But if this is your score, ask three or four of your associates to check the list for you. Then compare your findings with theirs. If your score is 100 or less you should be so physically well, so rested and relaxed, so joyous and successful, that everyone about you marvels at your buoyancy, your youthfulness, your wit and wisdom, the glorious dynamic of your personality. Whatever your score, your achievement, health and happiness in everyday life should be an evidence of the accuracy of your total estimation.

May I suggest that you list the ten highest ratings and think deeply on their significance? John Doe, for example, being a characteristic American, achieved the following high scorings:

Assume without assurances	6
Let work pile up	10
Become overworked	7
Often reconsider	9

Make effort at random	8
Sink into routine	9
Depend on luck	6
Feel you must compromise	9
Use guesswork for important things	8
Seldom feel relaxed	7

It is now wise to fill in an affirmative estimation, so that it may be compared with the negative findings to check and balance the final conclusion.

DO YOU:

#	Question	Scale
1.	Work at the job while you're on it	o 1 2 3 4 5 6 7 8 9 10
2.	Listen carefully to instructions	o 1 2 3 4 5 6 7 8 9 10
3.	Try again after failure	o 1 2 3 4 5 6 7 8 9 10
4.	Form conclusions carefully	o 1 2 3 4 5 6 7 8 9 10
5.	Think over the assertions of others	o 1 2 3 4 5 6 7 8 9 10
6.	Wait for second impressions	o 1 2 3 4 5 6 7 8 9 10
7.	Refuse to accept pressure	o 1 2 3 4 5 6 7 8 9 10
8.	Get work done on time	o 1 2 3 4 5 6 7 8 9 10
9.	Get results from ideas	o 1 2 3 4 5 6 7 8 9 10
10.	Find ways to avoid overwork	o 1 2 3 4 5 6 7 8 9 10
11.	Concentrate on primary values	o 1 2 3 4 5 6 7 8 9 10
12.	Develop incentive	o 1 2 3 4 5 6 7 8 9 10
13.	Stick to a decision	o 1 2 3 4 5 6 7 8 9 10
14.	Forget annoyances and go on	o 1 2 3 4 5 6 7 8 9 10
15.	Accept only what you can do	o 1 2 3 4 5 6 7 8 9 10

16.	Direct your effort logic-ally	o	1	2	3	4	5	6	7	8	9	10
17.	Correct things instead of excusing them	o	1	2	3	4	5	6	7	8	9	10
18.	Find ways to keep your freedom	o	1	2	3	4	5	6	7	8	9	10
19.	Get adequate rest	o	1	2	3	4	5	6	7	8	9	10
20.	Invent new ways	o	1	2	3	4	5	6	7	8	9	10
21.	Plan your work and work your plan	o	1	2	3	4	5	6	7	8	9	10
22.	Evaluate situations im-personally	o	1	2	3	4	5	6	7	8	9	10
23.	Distribute the burdens	o	1	2	3	4	5	6	7	8	9	10
24.	Estimate the qualities	o	1	2	3	4	5	6	7	8	9	10
25.	Measure the quantities	o	1	2	3	4	5	6	7	8	9	10
26.	Test the strengths	o	1	2	3	4	5	6	7	8	9	10
27.	Expose the supposi-tions	o	1	2	3	4	5	6	7	8	9	10
28.	Analyze the facts	o	1	2	3	4	5	6	7	8	9	10
29.	Investigate the pur-poses	o	1	2	3	4	5	6	7	8	9	10
30.	Discover who belongs	o	1	2	3	4	5	6	7	8	9	10
31.	Synthesize the details	o	1	2	3	4	5	6	7	8	9	10
32.	Remain alert	o	1	2	3	4	5	6	7	8	9	10
33.	Estimate the averages	o	1	2	3	4	5	6	7	8	9	10
34.	Interpret the trends	o	1	2	3	4	5	6	7	8	9	10
35.	Validate your decisions	o	1	2	3	4	5	6	7	8	9	10
36.	Objectify your ideas	o	1	2	3	4	5	6	7	8	9	10
37.	Concentrate on pri-maries	o	1	2	3	4	5	6	7	8	9	10
38.	Rate the secondary values	o	1	2	3	4	5	6	7	8	9	10
39.	Refuse to depend upon chance	o	1	2	3	4	5	6	7	8	9	10
40.	Form your own con-clusions	o	1	2	3	4	5	6	7	8	9	10

41.	Chart your way for important matters	0	1	2	3	4	5	6	7	8	9	10
42.	Work out your idea of true values	0	1	2	3	4	5	6	7	8	9	10
43.	Ignore petty irritations	0	1	2	3	4	5	6	7	8	9	10
44.	Go ahead with or without help	0	1	2	3	4	5	6	7	8	9	10
45.	Simplify to essentials	0	1	2	3	4	5	6	7	8	9	10
46.	Have your own sincere aims	0	1	2	3	4	5	6	7	8	9	10
47.	Practice relaxation	0	1	2	3	4	5	6	7	8	9	10
48.	Develop labor-saving methods	0	1	2	3	4	5	6	7	8	9	10
49.	Work on a philosophy of life	0	1	2	3	4	5	6	7	8	9	10
50.	Remain alert	0	1	2	3	4	5	6	7	8	9	10

The highest score that is possible is 500. This can only be achieved by a genius who is also a calm, poised and perfectly healthy individual. A score of 400 means that the person able honestly to make such a record has a remarkable command of his relation to life. A score of 300 is still unusual. If, however, your score is only 200, you are letting circumstances control your life. In such a case, ask three or four of your associates to check the list for you and compare your findings with theirs. If your score is 100 or less, you should see your doctor and also seriously reorganize your way of life. In fact, you need a great deal of help. Whatever your score, it should be evaluated in relation to the way you deal with your everyday life.

It is always wise to list the ten highest ratings and to think deeply about their significance, for you will find they delineate how you best use your attention. John Doe, for example, achieved the following high ratings:

Try again after failure	9
Get results from ideas	9
Direct your effort logically	8
Develop incentive	7
Find ways to keep your freedom	6
Invent new ways	9
Simplify to essentials	7
Go ahead with or without help	7
Develop labor-saving methods	6
Remain alert	10

Compare the ten highest negative ratings of John Doe with his ten constructive scorings. In such a finding there is a suggestion at least of our national weakness and our national strength. We let work pile up. We compromise essential values. We allow routine to rule our lives, while striving to endure the strain. At the same time, we are a remarkably alert people, seldom stopped by failure. We try again, objectifying our ideas and inventing new ways.

It is also wise to list the ten lowest scores in each test and to compare them as well as to study and compare all the negative and positive results. If your findings impel you to make more of your effort to get back to the reality of your true aims, it will prove its usefulness.

To achieve an approximation at least of how we live our personal lives is the second concrete step in the art of living without tension.

3 ADVANCED EFFORT

To APPLY modern techniques successfully, it is essential to consider to some degree their order of importance. We must begin with the principle of preparation. None of us will easily escape from helter-skelter living unless the habit of being ready for the experience we must deal with is firmly established.

All of the great therapies come from nature, the technique of advanced effort most conspicuously so. In every seed there is the design of the plant, vine or tree that is to be, with the entire plan of its life, and directions for its growth, carefully conceived in advance of its sprouting. If science and engineering did not also follow this wise procedure, neither would long exist.

Since most people in the ordinary events of life ignore this great process, they are subject to nervous effort when a task comes upon them. Advanced effort operates to avoid confusion, overlapping of action, deficiency at important points, and to make possible an adequate supply of energy. Each of us should organize a program of carefully designed behavior when dealing with serious matters.

Advanced effort is essential because life has become too complex for the simple process of doing the best one can when work is at hand. The average man a century or so ago could do his chores with little forethought because his tasks differed but slightly each day from the day before. Modern life is a series of unexpected challenges. For several decades I traveled thousands of miles every year. I knew that accidents were possible. I therefore conceived just how I would act if one came. Later, in a train wreck, I automatically did what I had planned to do and thus saved my life and those of others.

The more sides of experience you must deal with, the more you need to establish a series of plans as to how you will think, feel and act in the situations that are most likely to develop. It may even be wise in some cases to write out concise descriptions of your procedures, and conceive the details of your campaigns as a great merchant might plan his strategies. Does your wife unburden herself upon your return home from a hard day at the office? Then you need to decide in advance how you will keep cool. If you were deaf and dumb there could be no argument. You can, if you wish, behave as if you had that protection.

When a husband, for example, characteristically forgets how irritating and fatiguing a wife's day can be, dealing with the children, the shopping, the telephone ringing and the callers with their endless talk, a plan as carefully designed as a lawyer would prepare a case is essential for a housewife, if she wishes to maintain poise. It is useless to try to convince most men their days may be easier than those of the woman in their life, and that is why a well-planned self-control pattern is needed.

No businessman these days expects his industry to succeed unless all its activities are organized. An explorer before going into the jungle or up to the Arctic gives the most meticulous attention to what he is to take and what he is to do. Not even a moron attempts to build a hen coop with no plan. Yet most of us fail as architects of fate because we let the currents of destiny come upon us without any forethought whatsoever.

DEAR DR. SEABURY:

I cannot put into words what a complete change has come into my life since I learned how to apply Advanced Effort in my business. I have found concrete planning and thoughtful preparation especially useful. My shop manager is a good man, but a difficult one. Every so often he gets all steamed up, and has to blow off. That used to upset me so I couldn't sleep, and even anticipating such scenes put my nerves on edge.

You told me to try to achieve the same attitude a dramatist has when writing a play: an impersonal perspective, and a lively interest in the kind of antics a human being can create. I have learned to achieve that attitude, and it helps.

When I began to consider in my mind the way I'd act when my shop manager puts on a scene, and to imagine what I'd say and how I'd say it, I suddenly realized that many of these set-tos are almost exactly alike, and that I could establish my role and practice it until I'd be so skillful it would even be amusing to see each situation through.

It puzzles me though why these scenes come so seldom

33

now. Anyway, I wanted you to know I'm a wholehearted advocate of this way of automatic preparation.

Most gratefully,

RALPH C. B.

No sane person would suggest that anyone needs to use such methods all the time, or with everything he does. You have measurements made and a pattern cut before a dress or a suit is put together. But you do not have yourself measured every day you wear it. Designs are made for every part of an automobile before each element of it is constructed. When the machine is put together and running on the road, the designing is over. Once upon a time someone had to tell you how to eat porridge to keep it off your face and to get it safely into your mouth. Quite a little careful planning was then necessary. I doubt if you now need such disciplining to consume your meals successfully.

The point is that when one has designed his conduct by forethought, the nervous system becomes so constructively conditioned that it behaves in the right way automatically. Your nerves become trained in concordant behavior patterns so that your organism co-operates with ease and efficiency.

Many suppose that to take time to establish advanced effort adds one more task to an already crowded life. This is emphatically not so. It saves countless hours in the future and reduces the effort then expended to a minimum.

There was a time when it took effort for you to do some present task of yours that you now accomplish with ease. You have become familiar with its requirements. If you still lacked the necessary training patterns, and had to face your work afresh every day with no preparation, you would reach home —if you reached it at all—utterly exhausted and with nerves at the breaking point.

Yet in countless ways, in human relations especially, we

ignore completely the thoughtful preparation that could make things go smoothly, or at least less exhaustingly.

DEAR DR. SEABURY:

You recall that I have two very different children; the boy a potential genius with all the high tension that that means, and a girl who is just a little bunch of mischief.

You told me it was possible to learn how to handle such children, and not be so irritated and worn out by night that I wanted to die. Frankly, I didn't believe you, and for a long time my failure to apply what you told me proved to me that you were wrong.

Then one day I observed our colored cook while she quietly made both of my children obey her. Neither she nor they knew I was watching through the kitchen door.

"You all ain't gwine ter make fools o' yoselves in dis yere kitchen," she stated bluntly, "an' if yo' don't mind you ways de good Lord'll gib you de hebejeebees."

"What are they?" my son asked solemnly.

"De nerves dat jump up and down yo' spine like fleas on a dog's tail. Yo' can't avoid 'em lessen you learns to dis'plin yosef."

Both children were now standing by the ironing board as Mirandy talked. In her own colorful way of speaking she gave them a word picture of what good conduct was, why it should be striven for and how in advance they could see themselves behaving well and the satisfaction they could get from not causing the sort of trouble they disliked in others.

"Suppose yo' ma was up to mischief all de time an' had tantrums," she said slowly.

"I'd want to run away," my little daughter stated soberly.

"So would I," the boy agreed. "Only I'd be afraid to."

"Den yo' all both picher how yo' wants to behave, or yo' ma will git all wore out."

35

Mirandy didn't know it, of course, but she was teaching those children the very sort of therapy I'd refused to receive from you. But now I'm using it, and it works. I've studied both my children and found what their characteristic behavior problems are. Now I can meet the situations that arise. More than this, I've discovered some of the causes of their antics so that they don't happen as often as they did.

Penitently,

GRACE O. M.

If you will take a little time to list the things, the situations and the ways of the people that cause you trouble in life, and then think over how by advanced effort such situations could be met, you will have taken a great step toward easing out of strain. If you add to this the making of designs of the behavior you wish to establish in yourself, and some planning of what you feel it is wise to say, you will have taken a second step in the control of events. Thirdly, and most important of all, establish the thought in your mind that there is a center of strength in you which will automatically come into action to guide and tell you what to do and say. Even if you don't believe in your capacity for insight, try it.

Tell yourself that the good automatic habits you seek to establish will soon work without further attention from you, and as swiftly and easily as does your mother tongue. The language you speak is only a series of engrams, organized into groups, and the groups into verbal conduct patterns. Your ability to talk rapidly so as to express your thought is entirely the result of advance efforts that have become designed and habituated.

One time years ago I discovered I had to take a long horseback trip with four old cowboys. I'd never been on a horse in my life. Fortunately I knew of the trip five days in advance.

I didn't go out and try to act like a broncobuster in order to meet the emergency. Instead, I went to an auction stable where horses were constantly being tried out by expert riders. I watched day after day, returning now and again to my hotel room to lie on my bed and feel myself riding. When the great day came, I rode in just the way I'd seen those horsemen do. And what is more, I did it so well the cowboys never knew I was a tenderfoot. Actually I wasn't any longer a tenderfoot, was I? Hadn't I by hours of organized thought learned how to ride, just as if I had actually been doing it?

This information about automatic adjustments may not seem as valuable to you as an offer of precious nuggets. You may not have any more perspective as to such mental values than a cat has of a gold mine. But I know men and women who use organized thinking to develop all sorts of mental and physical skills. One of the great golfers became a champion because of it. His letter is in my files. One of the famous violinists developed his skill that way. I have his record too.

It has been the secret of many a successful public speaker. But more than that, it has been the way thousands have been able to give up old habits of self-consciousness, hesitation and failure and build conduct patterns of confidence, achievement and happiness. There isn't a single truth about your mind so important as the fact that you can train it to work for you automatically if your advance effort is earnestly made and felt with purpose and emotion. Gold nuggets, nonsense! They aren't half as valuable as this knowledge.

As you read on you will find that much of the material that follows contains methods of advanced effort put in the order of a step-by-step development of this great process. Each step leads into a deeper and deeper understanding and a more and more thorough use of the means by which we can all ease out of strain. Adanced effort is the third concrete step.

4 CONSTRUCTIVE LIVING

*S*UCH is the power of old habits that, unless we alert ourselves to their encroaching tendency, our new insights and purposes are soon destroyed and we are back again in the dull routine. This is especially the case in the use of any attempt to release our desires into good functional patterns. Unless we check ourselves and face the power of the "set" conduct that has controlled us, we are likely to lose the new vision and slip back into the toilsome routine.

For this reason those of us who have striven for years in clinical practice, or by means of books and lectures, to help our fellow man have found that we must patiently explain and dramatize the constructive ways of striving that lead to an easing out of strain.

Consider, for example, the life story of Bob Craige. Up to the time he became engaged to Alice Melden he had made little progress. He had, to be sure, graduated from school a valedictorian. An honor man in college, he had looked forward to a successful career upon completing his academic training. Financial necessity forced him to take the first job that offered. And there he stuck, unable to advance.

Success seemed to slip from his grasp. Nor was it only money he could not gain. His hope of a home of his own seemed impossible of realization. It was then that Alice came into his life.

"I want to help because I love you," she told him. "But it's more than that. You deserve to have your hopes realized."

"They never are," Bob complained bitterly.

"And they never will be unless you make them more definite. In college I specialized in mental hygiene, and I've found it no end of help."

"But how?" Bob's voice was tinged with skepticism.

"From learning to create in my mind all the aspects of whatever I want to come to pass, and to do it fully and thoroughly before I make any active moves."

"You mean you imagine what you want? That sounds like wishful thinking or daydreaming."

"It doesn't have to be. Would you say that a civil engineer was doing wishful thinking when he draws plans for all the details of the power lines of a city before the conduits are built?"

"Certainly not, but—"

"Let me finish. Would you say a composer was daydreaming when he creates the score of a symphony before an orchestra plays it?"

"That would be ridiculous." Bob sat forward as if beginning to see the light.

"It would be more ridiculous if a general in time of war

39

didn't organize his campaign before his soldiers were exposed to enemy fire. Yet, Bob dear, you've lived your life in quite as haphazard a way."

"What should I do?" he asked slowly, as if pondering his many failures.

"Whatever you want to have come to pass, and anything you wish to gain, should first be fully realized in your mind. Can you recall your own bedroom?"

"That's for sure."

"Can you see it and also mentally touch the objects in it?"

"You bet."

"Can you hear that little radio you have on the table near the south window?"

"O. K."

"Well, I could go on and on until we had mentally experienced every aspect of your room. Have you ever created in your mind the sort of house you want to have some day? I mean as clearly as we have realized your room?"

"No, I guess I've just not had time to do that."

"No." Alice's voice was brisk now. "Nor have you been definite about your other desires. You've lived your life as a man would who tried to build a house without any design, putting a window here, a door there, with no clear idea where the rooms would be, and no closet space planned at all. That's your trouble, Bob darling. You've plenty of brains and lots of ability, but it's all been unorganized."

"You mean that since I'm what they call an intellectual man I ought to have no trouble?"

"No, I mean that perhaps it is because you are called an intellectual that you do have trouble."

"I don't get you—you have me all confused."

"It's not your learning and your mental brilliance that will help you, Bob. But it is your imagination, your ability

40

to realize in your mind what you intend to do and wish to have, to picture it concisely and in detail. And let me tell you this: lots of so-called simple people do use their imaginations constructively and succeed in life because of it. It's also the secret of genius. Brilliant men often fail, but those who make plans and make them operate usually succeed."

Many are they who suppose that the way out of our modern morass is achieved by purely intellectual means. They would outsmart fate. Few, if any, achieve their aim. Intellectual power is essential to the acquisition of knowledge, but research and statistics prove that merely intellectual people are more unhappy than those with simpler minds. Sophistication too often leads to cynicism, doubt and despair. Cleverness assists only in the development of mental skills. Keen, critical powers, let us admit, are essential to the achievement of scholastic prowess and erudition. A brilliant man may speak a dozen languages and possess an encyclopedic mind. But he does not thereby avoid strain or have a life more comfortable than that of a moron.

The answer to this enigma is clear. It is found in the fact that it is man's sensory endowments, used as adjuncts to memory, reason and imagination, that give controlling power to personality. Intellectuality and judgment are essential, but they are devoid of creative energy unless motivated by a sense-quickened imagination. This fact is of major importance to anyone who wishes to live well. It is also the reason why many ordinary people have happier days than those of brilliant sophisticates. Many an apparently simple-minded farmer possesses great understanding. There are housewives who have innate wisdom.

Have you ever followed keen-eyed guides through the Canadian woods, and observed how adroitly they meet the difficulties that arise? Have you ever watched a group of explorers getting ready for an expedition? Memory, reason and imagination are at work. The expedition is designed by forethought. Memory assembles knowledge from the past. Reason selects what is needed in the present. Imagination looks to the future and then creates the blueprints that make efficient planning possible. Yet under it all are the sensory powers which give to these three formative attributes their ability to help us *realize* what is and what is not. That is an amazing word: *real - ize.*

Your memory is a poor instrument unless you have seen and can resee whatever things and facts you need to recall. You do not remember well what you have heard unless you can rehear it accurately. Unless your mind was touched by what you experienced and you can touch it in thought, little information that is valuable is remembered. Facts have small worth unless you can sense their formation. Information requires that one comprehends the formation. The form must be realized. So with the use of all other sensory endowments. Without the senses of taste and smell there would be no cooking skills, and but scant enjoyment in the act of eating.

Even the animals have sensory powers which give them pleasure and help to protect their lives. But they do not have equivalent capacities of memory, reason and imagination. It is these three gifts that add subjective power to the senses. They make it possible for you to visualize and revisualize your wants. From their use insight develops. Imagination, like a mighty instrument, is able to project clear-cut images of whatever you seek to acquire. Its use is a powerful and practical means of bringing a better future to pass.

In the last analysis, the design that results from such forethought is, or should be, a sensory equivalent of what one wishes oneself to become or to possess.

Such a sensory equivalent is a structural pattern in one's

mind that gives form and substance to one's desires. A young salesman listening thoughtfully to an "old hand" presenting his product may acquire in his mind the methods and feeling of that kind of salesmanship. He develops a sensory equivalent of the older man's action pattern which, if adhered to, can become a templet or guide to the establishment of the same efficiency in the young observer.

A boy, seeing on a motion picture screen how an accomplished actor makes love, may build a sensory pattern, or equivalent, of the actor's amative skill. This becomes a formative force in the boy's own development. Nor is a girl, identifying with the way the heroine is wooed, less adept at transferring to herself the behavior she sees on the screen. The sensory equivalent she creates of how to be loved becomes a powerful force in her own responses. It is in this way that all sorts of automatic conduct patterns become imprinted upon our impelling centers of thought, feeling and action.

A study of the behavior of those who lived dynamic or fortunate lives reveals that they invariably yet unconsciously created sensory equivalents of their desires and purposes. The word sensory, rather than mental, is used because these formative patterns are dramatizations of *feeling* as well as of thought. They are functional or doing designs, fashioned by touch, hearing, sight, indeed by all the senses.

When a boy watches a skilled aviator land or take off, and identifies with him, he creates sensory equivalents of the aviator's skill in which, as a man, he may later function. Men of great achievement seem to have instinctively or intuitively created sensory equivalents, not only for their own conduct to act in, but of all they desired in life. In other words, they identified themselves with conduct patterns that would so affect their relation to environment and the people in that

43

environment that success and good fortune were actually and literally brought to pass in consequence.

Here we have at last the secret which most of the great and near great used as their means of accomplishment. Mere energy is not the answer. Undirected enthusiasm fulfills few aims. An affirmative attitude too easily becomes a vapid optimism, dynamic organization is often a primitive selfishness; nor will a dauntless spirit that believes nothing is impossible lead to conquest, if it remains an unorganized belief.

Energy, enthusiasm, any and all of our passions and compulsions, must be given form and direction. They require constructive fulfillment which by means of repetition becomes habituated into deep-cut channels. Otherwise idle, delinquent, unwise and destructive release of these mighty forces is established and often made permanent.

The insight that was missing in the life of many a great genius lay in the fact that he had little knowledge of how he created and used the sensory equivalents that made the expression of his genius possible. He had even less understanding of how he could develop and use such a means of self-command in his more personal life.

How such templets of conduct are to be used leads us to an essential consideration. For great as is the power of sensory equivalents they will not succeed if created to do what cannot be done. Mirabeau and Napoleon to the contrary, there *are* things that are impossible, and intelligent living requires that they be discovered. This means, of course, that one must separate those aspects of life that are inevitable from those that are adjustable. Surrendering without protest to the inevitables, we must then concentrate on those adjustables that are important to us as individuals, creating as we do so sensory equivalents for their conquest. We must develop the behavior that will achieve our wisely selected goals. By this

44

means none of our surging power is suppressed, the dynamic flow is not stopped or the flame put out, use whichever metaphor you will. Our passions are released but directed, our energies are used. What, without adequate design, was but force within us is developed into constructive power. We become so dynamically and joyously busy doing what can be done, we have little sorrow for the restrictions of destiny.

The great Helen Keller most certainly had to accept the inevitability of her blindness and deafness. Yet by a majestic use of sensory equivalents she developed herself far beyond ordinary people.

Time spent in creating such functional patterns returns rewards beyond all usual efforts. Let yourself feel and feel passionately how you can so behave that your constructive desires will be fulfilled. They are achieved by you only when you have learned how to concentrate your dynamic energy upon them. Surrender yourself to the constructive habits that this persistent functionalizing of your longings brings to pass. Your habits will then become automatisms that carry you forward without the soul-grueling effort that is otherwise necessary.

The aim of all the modern means of conquest is the establishment of habits of thought, feeling and action that when well developed will function of their own accord and require no conscious effort in their use. Clinical psychologists hope to help everyone to do all he does as easily as he makes the motions that handle his car in traffic. You do not have to make a conscious effort to step on the gas or to turn the wheel. The wheel "becomes turned," the gas or the brake "goes on." If these activities did not "just happen" (once you have learned how to drive), you would be worn out in a week and your automobile become a useless vehicle.

Are you willing to contend that all that we think, feel and

do cannot, with training, be done as automatically as you drive a car? Do you insist that your thought life must be the same as that of man when he trod the earth with his two feet and had no other available means? Then you are among those who do not want and will not accept the modern ways of easing out of strain. You still worship routine duty, egotistical toil, and from a negative undercurrent in your thought and feeling you wish to circumvent and "prove" that the new methods fail. If, however, you are open-minded and wish to be more than exposed to good mental hygiene, you must realize that the effort you expend is for the purpose of establishing such good habit ways that your life is eased by the use of them. Effort is not abolished but it is used in a very different place, or as one wag put it, "We use effort to abolish effort." Is not that just what modern mechanics does? It took effort to invent and to make an elevator: *effort to abolish effort*. It took effort to invent a modern typewriter with its automatic response to touch typing: *effort to abolish effort*. It took effort to invent and make a telephone that carries messages for us instantly and across thousands of miles of otherwise weary journey: *effort to abolish effort*.

That is just what the modern therapies do. Once established, they automatically reduce the strains and the tasks of living to a minimum. But it requires effort to master them so that their action becomes automatic: *effort to abolish effort*.

One could hope that this fact will be so clearly seen that it produces an intellectual conversion to the new ways of living. The ease it establishes would then become stabilized. From it a positive faith would come to pass.

In this reference a most important point must be considered: what is a positive faith? How do we achieve a will to believe that the great therapies can become such automatic powers that they carry life for us and we no longer have to carry it? There is, as far as we know, only one way and that is to expose oneself long enough and ardently enough to the use of these therapies that they "get into the unconscious," just as the right way to operate a car gets into the unconscious. Repetitive effort produces habits, and habits once established allow us to function automatically within them.

Success then requires an actual desire to possess this invincible way of living, together with an adequate use of the new and better procedures.

To be able to use them well you must, however, make an effort to escape from the surface intellectuality that has for many decades now been one of the curses of our American way of life. You must, within yourself, restore your sensory power as well as gain a close relation to nature.

Our American culture, as well as our educational system, seriously neglects the use and protection of the powers of our pioneer ancestors. Upon those powers the very existence of this nation depended. The majority of our forebears were not men of great erudition. They were not intellectuals, nor yet smart sophisticates. Their minds were keen, but keen because of the exigencies that a rugged land created. Their senses were alert, for life or death depended upon their development and efficiency. All that passed before them was swiftly observed, clearly seen, attentively heard, deeply felt. This sensitivity to life was more apparent in the true pioneers, whose work it was to clear the forests and conquer the land. Yet even the dwellers in town and city were in no sense matured by textbook studies.

There is nothing wrong with the use of one's intellect if it is accompanied by the use of one's intelligence. No one should condemn those learning methods on which modern education so depends, except for the deficiency in sensory training and emotional maturation. For that neglect we are paying a bitter price. None of the mental techniques and therapies which cure mental disturbances and keep man out of strain work well unless an emotional response and a sensory awareness accompany and empower the intellectual process.

For this reason, if you wish to gain command of the means that reduce worry, tension and the exhaustion that accompanies them, take a little time each day to feel—feel what the room you are in is like—sense its atmosphere, see it anew in color and form, hear the sounds that enter into it, touch the objects, the textures, handle some of the things it contains. By becoming aware of fragrant odors, by sensing temperatures, by feeling the weight of objects, you awaken your sensory potentials, you become alive. This quickening you need to give reality to the equivalents of what you desire to have and to hold in your life.

The coming to life of the powers that gave strength to the thought and action of the pioneers will then empower your making of the productive equivalents of your desires. It will also strengthen your thought and give it functional energy.

This is the fourth step in the art of living without tension.

5 DESIGNING EQUIVALENTS

*I*T IS a strange fact that so few people seem to have understood the importance of designing in their minds the equivalents of their desires or have realized that they are not otherwise easily acquired. So that there can be no doubt in the understanding of anyone, therefore, as to just what such an equivalent is, it may be well that we describe it, analyze it and study its forms as definitely as possible.

It is not enough to say that an equivalent is a desire in one's mind of what one wishes to have happen, and of how one intends to bring it to pass. It is more than that. Nor is it only a plan or a clarified purpose, even if there is much of such an arrangement in its mental structure.

Such a design is beyond question a pattern in the mind that is so well formed, and so fully realized, that it gives force and direction to one's desires. But that is also not enough to say about it, for if that were all there is to it many people would long ago have made and applied sensory equivalents, achieving more of the things that each wished to accomplish. That has not been the case, which the prevalence of strain and worry proves.

To make our subject so clear that anyone can use equivalents in practical ways, let us consider a few cases of application. For years, Peter Paulson had led a frustrated life. The well-known inferiority complex seemed to have him in its grip. He felt shy, nervous and inadequate. In his thirty-second year he had the good fortune to find a clinical psychologist who believed in the efficient power of prepared forethought.

He explained to Peter just what a sensory equivalent is. "You know how poised and confident men behave," he pointed out. "You have observed what they say and what they do. More than that, you must feel that these successful men do not nervously pull themselves apart by constant self-inspection. They accept themselves as they are. They use what they have of brains and personality. In your case a sensory equivalent means to feel and then to act as these achievers do. See yourself, hear yourself, think yourself into the conduct patterns of successful effort. This means you realize and use a firm, full voice when you speak; that you see yourself with a kindly smile on your face; in fact, that you put on the manners of masterful men, even as one puts on a suit of clothes."

Some years before Peter Paulson received this practical help, he had consulted the type of analyst who only put him through hours of recall of the years of his unhappy boyhood It revealed to Peter why he was shy and felt so inferior. But it left him there. "I needed this constructive therapy," Peter told his patient wife. "This I can use. I can live inside of the sensory equivalents of what I want to become. You'll see me go forward now." And he did.

Nellie Maddern had long been an invalid. She wasn't sick

exactly: that is, the doctors could not discover that she had any regular disease. Yet she was far from well. Then came the day when one of her old friends came to make her biennial call.

"I'm all excited over the use of sensory equivalents," she told Nellie.

"Sensory equivalents!" Nellie smiled wanly. "What on earth are you talking about?"

"About something that can get you well and up and about—that is, if you want to live a healthy, active life."

"Of course I do." The irritable note in the patient's voice did not escape her visitor.

"Look here, Nellie, you know what it is to feel well and be well, don't you? You know how well people decide what to do and do it. Now a sensory equivalent is a feeling in your mind of what it is like to have and to be what you want to become. In your case, it would be a seeing, hearing, touching —yes, even tasting and smelling—of what it would be like to be well. Tasting food again, getting up to smell some lovely flowers, seeing yourself getting out of bed as you used to do when you were a child."

"But I'm so weak," Nellie expostulated.

"You are now, but you won't remain so if you feel the blood circulating through your veins and nurturing your cells. You can then begin to exercise a little—and more each day— until you gradually regain your strength. If you live in the equivalents of health, you will get well. Cast off the equivalents of sickness that have obsessed you for so many years and you'll be up and about."

So deep was Nellie's identification with weakness and disease that it took many visits from her friend to set the new pattern in motion.

"She's been psychosomatically sick," her doctor explained, glad of the co-operation that gradually brought her back to

51

health. "I wish we had more people to help such cases to cast off the equivalents of illness, and to realize the equivalents of health. That's the sort of medicine that is needed for a case like this."

It is not too much to say that the making of sensory equivalents in one's mind is the greatest means by which good fortune is brought to pass. By its use ill luck is as fully circumvented as is in each case possible. Our wishes, cravings and dreams come to fulfillment only when, in some measure, we have designed sensory equivalents of their realization. They may otherwise remain as mere fancies, vague longings and a wishful thinking so ineffectual that disappointment is inevitable. Upon the clarity and precision of sensory equivalents, formed by visualization and actively at work in one's thought, all achievement, comfort, usefulness, pleasure, skill and power depend.

The imagining and applying of sensory equivalents is not a new art. It is as ancient as mankind itself. It has always been used, but used in most instances so carelessly and haphazardly that much failure resulted. Nor is this all. For those of us whose work it has been to explain the importance of such equivalents have often had the experience of being repulsed when we have striven to show to others concretely and precisely what equivalents are and how to use them. We have also in many instances received but a halfhearted attention. So scant has the person's interest been that we are soon told he found little or no benefit from an application of the procedure.

This ineffective response is, we know, caused by the fact that our educational system and our social concept of achievement is built on the wrong basis. Instead of being shown how to learn with ease, we have been admonished by our supposed guides to toil for facts and to work hard. We have been told *what* to do, not *how* to do it without strain. Few, if any, of our monitors have explained that if we would design our doing in our minds by a sensory means, employing sight, hearing, touch and taste, we would save time and strength. Mistakes and confusion would also have thus been avoided.

There are those, of course, who will rush to tell you they have understood and used this means of planning all their days. To them it seems an old story. Maybe it is—in some fragmentary area of their lives.

Let us put it this way: the use of sensory equivalents has been known by millions in *theory*, but in *practice* only by those who accomplished their purposes. And even they did not know it as a means by which invincible living is made possible.

A mechanical draftsman will laugh you to scorn if you suggest to him that there is a principle, new to *him*, in the structural technique in which his work is engaged. You are not likely, however, to find him using it in his human relations. A builder of a dam might well insist that he would utterly refuse to erect the structure without the possession of an engineering plan. You may find that he has no such definite concept in his mind of how to construct his life. The designer of an engine undoubtedly has in his mind an operational equivalent of the machine he invents. He uses this concept constantly in each step of his task. But seldom has the same man an operation equivalent of how his love life can run smoothly, or his children be taught to develop.

Few carry a knowledge that is to them a commonplace in one field over to the other activities of their lives. Therein is the cause of disappointment, failure, unhappiness and most of the aspects of misfortune.

It is not wise then for a person to say that he understands and applies this greatest of life processes if he uses it vaguely, or only for one accomplishment. He does not understand it as the dynamic means of conquest unless he uses it as a dynamic means in all of life. It is not his mightiest tool if it lies idle in all but the doing of some single task.

He does not understand it if he does not know that by its use the control of fate is largely made possible. Nor indeed is he familiar with it until it has become his unconscious habit because of its repeated use in designing a fulfillment of his purposes.

It is not a process that should become a cumbersome self-consciousness. It is not a procedure that must be paused about and thought over just before anyone does anything. It should not remain as a purely conscious procedure. As a way of thinking, feeling and acting, it should become so ingrained a habit that its power in shaping results is spontaneous and a dynamic momentum. It should, when once established, work automatically.

Such an easy and smooth controlling of efforts and circumstances cannot, of course, be at first accomplished without repetitive effort, purposeful thought and conscious intent. The full and efficient application of sensory equivalents is an art that must be acquired. By the time you have read this book the knowledge of how to create and use sensory equivalents should be definitely and enduringly understood. That will be a mighty gain. Your life thereafter will become a destiny that is largely in your control. Ease will have overcome dis-ease in every area where such a conquest is possible. No sensory equivalents will, as we have said, ever achieve the impossible. That they can do all that *is* possible is enough, for it is many, many times more than most people ever realize.

Let us come to terms about this matter and, as clearly and fully as we can, study still more deeply exactly what a sensory equivalent is. There are six distinct kinds or varieties. First of all, there are those of what we want: that is, pictures of the *things* we desire, the plans of what we wish them to be like. These are designs of their form and structure.

Secondly, there are conceptions of *how* we can get our wants fulfilled; ideas as to the way we can gain our ends; arrangements for the acquiring, enjoying and using of whatever we love, are interested in and long to possess.

Thirdly, there are the clarified reasons for our definite conduct: *why* we must do what must be done to achieve this or that special aim. These are realizations of the causes that produce efficient behavior. They are purposive patterns of personal expression established for the control of effects by obedience to the cause of good fortune. Having thought about why we should do our doing in certain ways, we thereby create *operational* equivalents to direct our activity.

Fourthly, there are the rearrangements of circumstance because of *who* we are and who is involved in our purposes. This includes the affect of our desires on people and on situations. Since most modern environments are composed of our associates more than objects of nature, and our actions produce reactions in others, we should remember that our feelings arouse good (or bad) emotions in them. How we think and act is a stimulus to how they think and act. In large measure it determines their response to us. The kind of behavior they exhibit who are in our life pattern will in most instances help or hinder us in gaining their co-operation. Thus we need equivalents in our minds of how we will so act as to win their assistance rather than their hindrance.

It must be evident that all we desire and do comes to pass in certain places and that some spots for achievement are better than others. Such a selection also includes a decision as to what part of any task, object or program requires our attention. If a man wishes to lift water from a well, he must find out how deep the well is and how long a rope to fasten to his pail. An equivalent of the *where* must be in his mind if he is wisely to direct his activity.

This mental picture of the wheres constitutes the fifth form of this magnificent controller of destiny. Lastly, come the thought patterns as to the *time to act*, the equivalents so arranged that they will come spontaneously into play at the right moment to meet the shifting flow of events. I know that after fifty years of public speaking I would by now be worn out if I had had to make effort to meet each situation as it came along in the vicissitudes of a lecturer's career.

For all those years I have had well-established sensory equivalents, not only as to what I would say, but how I would say it. I also realized why I must use this or that behavior from a realization of whom I was addressing. To this pattern I added automatic designs as to *when* those equivalents of the results I desired would come into action. In other words, sequences were created because of who *I* am and why they who would listen had come to hear me. After this the timing was established. Since audiences differ I had also to consider where my thought, feeling and activity were to take place. All these factors then became activated by each lecture audience. The desired consequences then came to pass *when* needed.

Thus a whole series of response patterns became organized for, let us say, the way my mind was to function when a question period developed at the end of a talk. Almost as if some mighty genie were at work in me, this configuration of equivalents of question answering worked automatically, almost as if someone else, or some power inside of me, were doing the thinking and speaking. Believe me, I know in every nerve of my being the way such a procedure can become the greatest of blessings. It paid immeasurable dividends for what little time and effort it took to establish such efficient automatisms.

When as a child you first went to school, do you recall

what a long distance it seemed from your home to your classroom? Then, after you became familiar with the way to go, the schoolhouse did not seem far at all. Successfully to establish good sensory equivalents for all the activities of your life and the fulfillment of your desires, as you read my description of the procedures, may have seemed to be a long and difficult task. The method may appear complicated and possessed of so many aspects it may seem hard to master. This is not the case, and you will find—as you did concerning the distance to school and the time it took to get there—that the whole process of establishing smooth-working sensory equivalents is simple, and swiftly accomplished.

One of the reasons it becomes easy and does not consume a long period of effort is because you soon quite unconsciously begin to apply the process of making these equivalents to the learning of how to make them. Thus the effort becomes increasingly more effortless. You will find, for example, that just from reading this chapter a wanting to think, feel and act with ease becomes so intensified that the process is already started.

In any case, functional patterns have now formed as to what this efficient automatism is. By its use other equivalents are made possible. It is already at work in your mind. Isn't it? Then let it work. Don't force it. Long to have it work. Crave to possess the ease and the increased power that is thus made yours. If you let it come, it will do so of itself.

As I have previously explained, we do not use the term mental equivalents, because the structure of which an equivalent is formed must possess concreteness and functional efficiency. Even the senses of smell, taste and temperature are sometimes part of such a design. No woman buys the right perfume for her personality, or knows how to wish for it successfully, if she has no odor equivalent in consciousness.

No one—man or woman—is ever a good cook who has not well established taste equivalents in mind to guide the combinations that are created. No composer ever wrote great music, or any virtuoso ever played it well, who did not possess resonance equivalents for every combination of sound the musical score involved.

When the advertiser of a lotion speaks of "the skin you love to touch," he is appealing to a tactile equivalent already latent in you. He is asking you to realize in your mind the thrill you would receive if you stroked the face of a woman who uses his cosmetic—or, if a woman, of being so stroked.

When you use such a process imaginatively—in your own mind, realizing objects, forming pictures and living in the activities of what you yourself wish to do or say, adding to it whatever of the other vividnesses are needed—you are creating the most powerful of operational equivalents. They can, if you let them, work automatically for you. They are doing-decisions, shall we say, purposive patterns that possess structural power. They then create actional responses in your brain and even in your nervous system and glandular organism. You are thereby constructively set in motion.

Such designs are in a sense momentum generators, since they induce energy and use your enthusiasm dynamically. In fact, the more fully you let your passion flow into these templets of accomplishment the more power they possess. Your emotions then become e-motions, motions out of you into the adventure of achievement. Success is then compulsively brought to pass by a spontaneous yet fully directed impelling.

There is no possession so magnificent as a well-established momentum of sensory equivalents.

The question is often asked: "How can I apply this procedure to my own life?" The answer is simple. You do so by considering who you are and what you want. You apply it by calmly surveying your present circumstances to see what opportunities, as well as what limitations, are involved in the tenor of your life. It is done by considering what in your environment and the people in it are compatible to you. You must consider what conditions are adequate for your growth and achievement; and what changes must be made if your life is to gain satisfaction. There is much that you can give to the world in which you pass your days. There should also be much that you can take from your environment, because it belongs to you by the edict of nature. Even as a plant must have adequate sustenance or die, even as any and every animal has its needs that must be met, so you have your rights and your requirements.

Your sensory equivalents can and should be conceptions in your mind of the fulfillment of these rights and requirements, as well as the conduct ways you should follow that will most successfully bring them to pass.

If you are unmarried and desire romance as well as the fulfillments of love in a home and children, hold in your thought the vital concepts of romance, love, children and a home. These concepts will, if vivid enough, act like guideposts to direct your way of life toward fulfillment in marriage. But if you also have in your mind the sensory equivalent of what loving behavior is, how a spirit of companionship functions and how kindness, thoughtfulness and nurture of others are formed and expressed, you will shape your behavior so that almost without effort, and even spontaneously, you will be bringing the love and marriage to pass. There is no one so desirable as he or she who has learned how to give and to receive love.

The spontaneous use of equivalents for the fulfillment of your life purposes and needs is the fifth constructive step in the art of living without tension.

6 YOUR WILL TO ACHIEVE

*I*T IS not enough to know that sensory equivalents are clear diagrams of what we wish to possess and of what we must do to possess them. It is beyond question that they are templets by which we hope to shape the future. But the problem now arises as to *how* such equivalents are most efficiently created and so developed as to become determinators and achievers of our constructive purposes. Nothing has formative power until the *how* of its realization is adequately developed and concretely used. In self-management this has been a sadly neglected fact.

The great accomplishers, in endeavoring to explain their success in life, have had more to say about the will than about any other attribute of personality. To most of them achievement seemed to be the result of saying, "I will," and sticking to it persistently. Epictetus, centuries ago, stated bluntly: "Freedom and slavery—the one is the name of virtue and the other of vice, and both are acts of the *will*."

Such a statement sounds more practical than it is. So also with the conclusions of La Rochefoucauld. "Nothing is impossible," he insisted; "there are ways which lead to everything, and if we had sufficient *will* we should always have sufficient means." He does not bother to tell us how we may develop sufficient will—a rather important point surely.

There is no question but that Disraeli was a great leader, but one wonders if everyone could achieve his success by applying his aphorisms. "Destiny bears us to our lot," he tells us, "and destiny is perhaps our own will." Beaconsfield was also most confident of man's power to overcome obstacles by the use of the will. "If we cannot shape our destiny," he concludes, "there is no such thing." Even the gentle Emerson believed deeply in a human capacity for conquest. "Art and power will go on as they have done, will make day out of night, time out of space and space out of time." No better prophecy of the great engineering achievements that have come since Emerson's day has ever been written. But does he tell us what the art of attaining this power is? That riddle has been left for our own time to solve.

The average person unfortunately still thinks that the setting in motion of the power of accomplishment is just an "act of the will." He believes that one decides what to do and then forces himself to do it. That is a major cause of misfortune in the average person's life. He does not realize that in one sense there is no such attribute as the will. Even as *attention* is a result of a union of many intellectual and sensory processes working together, so the will is an urge of one's protoplasm: a union of passion, enthusiasm and all the impelling and compulsive aspects of one's being. As such it is an *unorganized* force, a *latent* energy, but in no sense an actual strength until it is controlled and unified into a useful form.

We should think of the will as if it were a river having many tributaries, and possessed of a persistent flow; and, again like a river, an energy that must be given structure to possess power. Have you seen the long flumes in a country like Switzerland, where hydraulics is one of the national sciences? Each pipeline is a means of turning the forces of a stream into organized power.

Just such an engineering process is essential in human life if one would develop his will constructively. The pattern-making force of a plan, the directive efficiency of an idea, the organizing capacity of a purpose—alone give useful energy to the will.

If you grit your teeth, clench your fists and say, "I will," as a means of achieving anything, you probably won't. You only create strain. If you attempt to coerce yourself, as if only by a flagellation of your spirit could you possess volition, fatigue will overcome you in the end. Articles, pamphlets and books full of tush have been written about the use of the will, as if only by sticking out a great jaw could anyone succeed at anything.

In contrast to this abysmal nonsense, we know today that if you make dynamic designs in your mind of how you wish to behave, your will, like an invincible current, pours into the patterns you have created and gives you a magnetic vigor for the fulfillment of your desires. *The will obeys the thought patterns or mental images in your mind and operates as they command.*

Nowhere in nature are the forces of life harnessed to accomplish the special wishes of man. The tides come and go, the brooks and rivers flow, the sun pours energy upon the earth, steam issues from a geyser, myriad potentials appear, but few are in a form already adapted to man's use.

Life has also been generous to man himself in the matter of endowing him with flooding emotions, dynamic longings and an urge in his very glands. We should remember, however, that all this surge is only a protopathic thrust, only the potentials of volition. No man is born with will power. It is an accomplishment of training and design.

This dynamic strength is developed by making conscious or unconscious equivalents in one's mind of the ways that such a vigor can increase and operate. It is the product of one's urgings (libido, élan vital) united by the use of organization and structure. A man with a strong will may have inherited much *force* in his nature without which no such power could have developed. He may also be quite unaware of how he turned this force into a masterful volition. But whether he knew the process or not, its accomplishment depended upon formative planning to give coherence to his impelling.

More than seventy-five years ago an American by the name of Charles Godfrey Leland, living in Florence, Italy, wrote a book called *The Mystic Will*. In it he explained how to use what is now called the image-making process. He told what it could do to help one create will power in an efficient way.

While sojourning in Europe, William James came upon this book. He believed that the lesson it taught him saved his life. Never having had a strong constitution and with a heart always ready to "act up," he understood the importance of mentally picturing his behavior instead of using self-coercion. Those who knew James in his personal life remember how religiously he followed the method Leland had laid out, visualizing in a most definite manner how he wished his mind and body to function, then saying to himself, "Tomorrow, quite without effort, I shall do more and more this new way."

It is possible that not all his friends or family knew of this most private therapy, for James rightly believed that when we talk to others about such techniques we make ourselves self-conscious, and then that others are injuriously watchful for results. He knew that the "more and more this way" attitude was an essential easing out of any condition, and that a nervous expectancy as to results often denies them. The process needs faith not coerciveness to develop what it can do.

Is it not extraordinary that such a dynamic and efficient method of accomplishment should have been known for many decades and not have been recognized and used by everyone? Is it not stranger still that many of those who have known of this means of easing out of strain have failed to use it? Nor could anything be more amazing than the fact that few who have tried to use it have succeeded. What is the cause of this failure? It stems from the fact that to break down our habits of intellectual toil we need to have the power of this process presented to us again and again for the value of its use to become a conviction. William James knew this truth and emphasized it by saying that one had to have "the will to believe" in such methods for them to become used—or useful. A conviction is faith put in action—attention so merged with intention that purpose is empowered enduringly.

For the sake of emphasis and to help create a conviction as to the value of this great therapy, let me repeat and again repeat what I have said as to its formative usefulness.

First, let us fully realize that there is nothing new about the technique of imagery, and that it is not just another method to use in place of sensory equivalents. Rather is it a means of creating them with ease. Mankind did not invent this way of directing one's conduct. Research even in the field of biology has proved that an electromagnetic design precedes the development of all form. We need repetitively to realize that nature creates the architectural patterns of everything that lives, long before the structure comes into being. It is by this means that varieties and species are differentiated.

Unless in the nucleus of every reproductive cell there was the design of ultimate being, there could be no orderly unfoldment and no consistent growth. Nor is it only form and structure that this imagery creates; time of all sorts is an included factor. An annual plant has in its seed the duration of its life. So too has a perennial. In it is its age span, and its growing rate.

The principle is also clearly evident in many of the activities of man, and especially so in this scientific age. The work of a mechanical draftsman in an engineering activity is, as we have said, for the purpose of objectifying the design of a machine before a single part is made. But it is also used to determine the exact measures, shapes and relation of each and every element. An engineer would consider it madness to proceed with the structural processes until the drafting was complete. Most changes in design take place at this preliminary stage and not when material is being used.

Even in mechanics, however, the image-making process is first subjective: a creative designing in the mind of a construction engineer. Orderly imagination is at work in his thought.

Especially is this visualization at work in the mind of an inventor and upon the fullness and clarity of his imagery the success of his creation depends. For it to work well his thought must be functional: a conception of operations in full embodiment, not an abstract speculation in words. This deliberate procedure pertains to the way image-making should be used in the direction of human conduct. The more definite one's design of how he can and will meet some problem, the more successfully and quietly it is met.

Many of the leaders of men have strongly realized the

formative vigor of imagination, without exactly knowing why it is so powerful. As with their ideas about the will, they admired imagination and admonished others to believe in it. But they left the matter there. "Imagination rules the world," cried Napoleon. "Imagination disposes of everything," wrote Pascal, "it creates beauty, justice and happiness, which is everything in the world."

But how? They did not say.

Henry Ward Beecher went so far as to state: "The soul without imagination is what an observatory would be without a telescope," adding that "Faith is nothing but spiritualized imagination." Great as such truths are, they leave us without the information we need to use such knowledge.

Some of the more thoughtful minds, however, came a little nearer to practical truth. George Elliot wrote: "We are all of us imaginative in some form or other, for images are the *brood* of desire." Bulwer-Lytton carries us still nearer when he advises us: "Never seek to represent the positive truth but the idealized *image* of a truth." To this Sallust adds: "Every man is the architect of his own fortune."

None of these thinkers, however, saw the importance of imagery to create the function of the will. Shakespeare came near to it when he wrote: "This is an art which doth mend nature—change it rather, but art itself is nature." Nevertheless, he did not state that it is far easier to change nature if one first conceives a method of how to do so. This important point was better understood by Samuel Johnson, who said: "Many things difficult to *design* prove *easy* to perform."

To explain this fact, we should remember the potent phrase: *"The will obeys the image in the mind."* In other words, will, as we have said, does not become useful until it is given patterns of conduct by visual imagery through which to operate.

The reason then for the importance of design consists in the fact that throughout the universe no true power appears until the designations of purpose have created ways and means by which such an end is realized. There is an impressive will to live and to grow in both the animal and vegetable kingdoms. Each is gifted with an impelling power of resurgence. But from first to last, in the original impulse to develop and in the determination to repair whatever injuries have taken place, methods, definite means or designs, that are equivalents of the desired form, in every case exist. They concentrate and direct the forces of change to definite ends and specific purposes.

He who realizes that he loses nothing by whatever time he takes in creating purposive imagery gains much, for he develops volitional mastery. There are those who do not want to take the trouble to develop self-command; the lure of self-indulgence is too strong and the effort to achieve self-direction seems too great. Such persons pay and pay for this delinquency, for nature is inexorable. After a while they lack the strength to deal with life and its problems overcome them.

There is no way to peace except by the use of formative thought, and let us say again, upon such a formative process the power of the will depends. When one must have strength to deal with difficult situations, this will power becomes a primary need.

If you are willing to drift through life as a neutral creature, escaping its pains but missing its joys, you do not require a functionalized will. You can cling like a parasite to some sturdier nature. But if in the tomorrows ahead of you you wish to live life fully and to play a dynamic part in it, you must organize your will. You do so by transmuting your urgings into definite imagery and clear-cut design, that they may be turned from undifferentiated force into organized power.

Time and place are always interrelated and they often merge, the wheres determining the whens, and the whens clarifying the wheres in which volitional effort should be expended.

Reduced to a simple equation, one might say that there are always places in any situation that are too set and too invincible to yield to any human instrumentality. But there are also many more places (and they are often revealed by the uncertainty of others and sometimes by adversaries), where one's unflinching determination changes the whole situation. The tide of battle has often shifted because a general saw such a spot in the enemy's structure and made swift use of it.

Even as image-making added years to the life of William James, so it can for you make as great a difference as would appear in the work of an engineer who had previously tried to manufacture machines with no designing or pattern making, in contrast to the quiet efficiency he would possess when he always had the fullest plans long before structural operations began.

We in the field of therapeutic psychology are not asking you to do anything strange. We are only suggesting that in an engineering age you must engineer your life if you wish to maintain your health.

For the sake of emphasis, let us repeat then that mental imagery as a human therapy is a process of visualizing how you wish to behave in definite situations. It is also a portrait-making activity in one's mind of the fulfillment of one's desires. It is a graphic series of mental descriptions of precisely how one will later on think, feel and act in order to bring those desires automatically into being. In using this process one creates new habit ways of thought, feeling and action that then work spontaneously in bringing to pass corrections and improvements in his life: clear sensory equivalents of conduct that are related to probable courses of action. These channels of habit then control one's behavior. Effort has been made to avoid effort.

Those who have failed in the use of this therapy did not realize that such images do not function automatically when they are not deeply felt: that is, made as real as a realization of life itself, and motivated by strong emotion. Thinking about an image or a series of them is not enough. You must yield yourself to them as a boy does when he reads an adventure story. An image is, in fact, a series of coherent reflexes working together, and as such it is a design capable of controlling the activity of the nerves and the functioning of the viscera. It must be concrete enough to accomplish that physical effect.

Without imagery one's good intentions are lost in a maze of vague longings. Mental imagery is emphatically not fantasy or wishful thinking. It is not a musing and a dreaming of what one desires, nor yet a mere affirmation or a mystical demonstration. Those are occult ways of doing. Mental imagery is precise and down to earth. It is the means by which one's longings acquire a form capable of bringing them to pass.

By this procedure we not only give substance to our own needs, but produce such a sense of purpose that other people feel its impelling influence. They then become (unconsciously) part of what we are designing. Here is a key to many of life's successes, and the reason some people live fortunately. The mental imagery of their way of life is so impelling, it stimulates response patterns in all who play a creative part in their lives.

This process of visualization then can be best used when

designing what one wishes to do and have come to pass. Mere luck is a delusion, and often an appearance only. He who by mental imagery has built dynamic patterns of his conduct, ahead of activity itself, *seems* lucky because he uses and controls the luck he has. Without this "engineering" no continued good fortune is possible. We are living in a material world. For this reason our desires must have equal structure or they cannot move the solid earth of physical experience.

Imagery produces its best results where planning has designated the *place* where effort is to be made. Life is full of currents, trends, motions, changes, evolutions and devolutions. The flow of destiny is an inevitable series of progressions and regressions in the transition of events. Places clearly appear where something needs to be done to change the direction of the flow so as to control the outcome. Thoughtfulness reveals where these applications of imagery are to be posited. Misfortune is reduced in consequence.

Within you there is a latent will to win which is quite as strong as your will to believe that you can. An affirmative attitude is the product of an inherent faith in the latent hunger in your nature, a hunger and thirst after fullness of life. Dynamic organization results from a thoughtful experimenting with this craving. A determined drive cannot be forced to come to pass. You cannot will to will. You will will to will if you *let* yourself will. That is not a funny phrase, but a major truth. Your will is an innate, impelling dynamic, a surge that forever pushes within you. When you restrain it, you make strain. When you withhold it, you make tension. When you fail to use it, you create exhaustion. You did none of these things as a child. You had plenty of energy, of desire or urge, and of *will* in consequence.

The children of good fortune are those who remain as children at heart. Becoming mature in mind, they learn to keep and to organize the urge that was theirs in youth. That this dynamic surge when released is dangerous, unless it is used constructively and thoughtfully organized, we admit. You see evidence of this resplendent power, sometimes well directed, sometimes in wild release, in the lives of the geniuses. But should we fear this kinship with Hercules because it is not always staid and sober? No, because by constructive contemplation we can learn so to organize our volitional strength that it becomes invincible power.

The use of imagery is the sixth step in the conquest of strain.

7 THE STRUCTURE OF ACCOMPLISHMENT

A CAREFUL study of the lives of the great achievers reveals the fact that they had an enduring loyalty to their longings and also a persistent repetitiveness. The secret apparently was not alone in the having of an innate impelling, but in a continuance of that impelling in certain directions and for unchanging aims. They so loved their interests that an ultimate fulfillment of their desires seldom flagged. If it did it was only to give them a respite while their reservoirs of energy became refilled. Soon they were back again, more impelled than ever by a consuming purpose.

It is a significant fact, however, that energy becomes disbursed and disappears unless it is given definite confines. The steam that rises from the spout of a teakettle has no strength. It develops power only when encased in a boiler and directed through pipes into the cylinder of an engine. The flash of ignited gasoline is without useful energy. It disappears into space. Vaporized and drawn into the engine of your car, it pulls you with the power of many horses.

To develop and to use such power in one's own life requires that we learn to adapt it to our needs. This means, of course, that we see and feel ourselves in precise situations and by this means connect our energies with the problems with which we have to deal. You may not care to possess the drive for religious beauty that consumed Michelangelo as he lay dressed only in a loincloth, painting the Sistine Chapel. Perhaps you do not especially wish to spend your life following the example of a man like Einstein. You are willing to let any scientific man analyze the curve of space and apply relativity to the fourth dimension. But plenty of the immediate values of life may be yours, and concern you intensely.

How then shall you most successfully develop mental imagery that will so harness energy as to give you the power you need for personal achievement? How can you most easily visualize those structures that will give form and substance to your plans and purposes? Is there any activity with which you are already familiar which can help you?

Let us consider one that is within the reach of practically everyone. There has probably been no single activity for many years past with which people in civilized countries are more familiar than with motion pictures. For decades they have held the attention and aroused the emotion of millions of the world's citizens. It is doubtful, however, if many of these same people have ever realized that the motion picture, and its emotional appeal, has in it a principle that when applied to a person's use of his mind exemplifies one of the greatest means of achieving health, happiness and success.

As you sit in a motion picture theater the activities of life are portrayed before you. Events come and go, crisis after crisis arrives and is solved or avoided. Life stories are revealed.

The play has a theme and narrative. The plot unfolds in a dramatic action. Heroism and cowardice appear, determination and hesitation move through the scenes. Most important of all, each major moment leads to a satisfactory conclusion, a "denouement" as it is called. Thought, emotion and action lead to a given end.

Most of us at one time or another have lived through similar attributes of such dramas as are put upon the screen. Were this not so, a motion picture would have no sense of reality and even less emotional appeal. We project our own lives into the pictures we behold, seeing and feeling what we have done and what we would like to do. This projecting of ourselves into such dramatic actions is a key to personal conquest. Each of us can learn to use it with all its dynamic emotional effect and to use it now.

Sit back and close your eyes for a few moments. As you do so, imagine that a motion picture is before you in which *you* are playing the lead. Let your emotions rise and go into the picture. It should be a portrayal that concerns some special desire of yours, a drama about some longing you greatly wish to have fulfilled. Picture it happening with you yourself playing intensely in it: that is, heroically conquering the difficulties in the way. Visualize just how you will deal with the greatest of obstacles in your way. Hear yourself speaking to those who need to be quietly put in their places. Live in this motion picture every evening for a while before you go to sleep. Live it with full emotional and sensory response. Go back every night to the same picture. Re-create it. Improve it. Add conclusive touches here, shorten it in the places that move too slowly. Work at it as faithfully as a scenario writer would in order to give you a dynamic picture.

There is, of course, more than one great desire you wish to accomplish. You may be in love and want to win the "only one" for yourself. You may also desire sufficient success and to win the money that would make marriage possible. You also can have a number of other important aims that are essential to your future health and happiness. Do not dramatize them all at once. Consider each by itself and create a motion picture in your mind of how each one of your desires is to be accomplished, one at a time. But in each case let your emotions flood into each act and each scene. Give to them all the feeling you have. Give it wholeheartedly and with a sense of surrendering your ego to the better ways of life that you are visualizing.

Hal Roldorf had been unsuccessful for years, not in his work only but in his whole life. It was as if the demon of frustration had him in its clutch. You know how it is when whatever you do seems to bring no reward that compensates for your effort. Believing the old adage that patience is sure to win, Hal had risen early, plodded on without complaint and seldom reached home except by a late commuting train. Then a change took place that transformed his life. It came in the guise of a visit from his older brother. Jim surveyed Hal's day, then said, "I want to tell you something, Hal. It seems to me that you're wearing yourself out, struggling blindly to get ahead. You apparently still believe the tush we've been taught about the sure reward of endless effort and faithful toil. It may have been true in our great-grandfather's day. It isn't now."

"But what else can I do, Jim? I don't know which way to turn."

"Then stop trying to turn this way and that. Stop and think instead. I took you to a motion picture show last night, you remember?"

"Yes, I enjoyed it, but what's that got to do with the doldrums I'm in?"

"It has a great deal to do with it. What you saw on the screen was visual imagery, wasn't it?"

75

"You mean that no people were actually there?"

"Yes, something like that. And you heard voices from a sound track, but no one near or behind the screen made a sound."

"Okay, but what—"

"Wait a minute, Hal. Let me speak. First of all the picture was a visualization of thought, feeling and action, organized so as to portray a definite purpose. The whole play was a design, a kind of functioning program. Now just such an action pattern—a purposeful plan I mean—should move in everyone's mind if he is to accomplish things successfully. You haven't been doing that. But I have; that is, I have since I attended those lectures I spoke of. And since then I've succeeded."

The two men talked long into the night. Jim pictured his brother's years of unplanned and unorganized effort driving him in obedience to the routine tasks put upon him by his so-called "superiors." He helped Hal to realize he had carried on no campaign for progress within his own mind. He got him to realize he could make motion pictures with his imagination, in which he repetitively visualized how he was to achieve the comfort and ease for himself and his wife and children that he had so long desired.

"What do you love to do most, Hal? What would give you the greatest satisfaction?" Jim asked quietly.

"Experimenting. I love research. I like to puzzle out mechanical improvement. But I have no time or—"

"Yes you have, but you haven't believed it. And the time to start is now."

Hal quite spontaneously began to create in his mind a veritable motion picture of how he would like to live and work. As a result he established a little experimental laboratory in his cellar, and two years from that time came up with improvements on several of the processes of the company for which he worked. For this effort he was not only compensated with money, but, because to pay him for what the new processes were worth would cost the corporation too much, he was made a member of the firm.

Matthew Dalton's drama was founded on a very different story. Matthew was deeply in love with a girl so beautiful and popular that he lived in constant fear she would soon marry someone else. She would have, too, had Matthew not become so nervous and depressed that he was forced to consult his physician. After he had blurted out the whole story the kindly old doctor, with a hand on the young man's shoulder, spoke somewhat as follows:

"You've been to plenty of motion pictures, haven't you, Matthew? Of course you have and you've seen skillful actors making love to beautiful girls. Now I want you to sit by yourself for at least half an hour every night, visualizing how you intend to talk, act and express your love for Helen. Make it seem real. Live in it. Give yourself to the visualization. Plan how you will speak to her and how you will show your ardor. Then tell yourself that that is the way you will be impelled to behave when you are with Helen. Don't just do it mechanically. No one makes love successfully that way. But picture yourself as spontaneously affectionate and unable to keep from expressing your adoration. Turn your feeling free until you believe in it, then live up to it when you're with Helen."

Matthew listened with all his senses and did as he was told. Not only that, he won Helen and *kept her love*. For, unlike so many men who become mere husbands after they marry, Matthew kept on being a lover.

Education has in recent decades come more and more to realize the importance of visualization. Boys and girls are now taught to make their studies more actual, more real and functional by picturing in their minds the activities, processes and structures of what they study. Years ago, when little tots were told that two times two make four, they often wondered what the words meant. Two what and two what made four? They needed at first to put together with their hands two little objects and then two more such objects to realize what two times two meant. Later on the visualization process could be used, supplanting the physical process and thus broadening the scope of the child's mind. But unless the visualization process actually developed, their learning became confusing and difficult. In such a case when they reached high school education became a dead subject, a matter of memorizing dates. But if they had learned to visualize the factors of every subject, from battles to the fine arts, to visualize the functional activities that brought civilization to pass, history would have become as vital and as real as the events in their own day and age.

Aware of the intense importance of visualization as a factor in learning, modern education has developed what is called the audio-visual method: that is, a functional presentation by the use of projecting instruments to appeal to ears and eyes as a means of reaching the student's brain, and as a more powerful method than that of reading the written word.

This emphasis on the concrete efficiency of sight and sound is just as important in adult life, and in the progress you and I can make, as it is in the schooling of our children. Take time to visualize what you wish to do and what you wish to possess before you do anything physical about it, or make any actual effort to gain it. See what you want in your mind as clearly as you observe a motion picture. See not only vivid and definite forms of your desires, but see yourself in action, in thought and with emotion doing things in a way that will gain your ends. Hear yourself saying the things that should be said so that others will wish to help you bring your desires to pass.

78

By so doing you will not only form constructive behavior patterns but clarify more fully your goals. But you will do more than this. You will begin to create useful and constructive dramas in place of the injurious ones in which so many people waste their strength.

A constructive change takes place in the life of anyone who realizes that few of us actually live true lives. Most everyone plays a part. He acts in a drama circumstance has forced upon him. He did not create the role he plays or the tragicomedy in which he speaks and acts. It came into being from the influence of the home, his associates and the social order. Experience, often of an unfortunate nature, has set the stage. He has become conditioned by the training patterns and the moral precepts that have descended from centuries of psychological ignorance.

You can, if you will, take a little time to analyze your life and to study the part you play in it. If your role is not a successful and a happy one, you can gradually refuse longer to play the part you have so long suffered. You can also change your seeming fate: first, by refusing to believe it is your inevitable destiny, and second by gradually conceiving quite a different drama.

Consider, for example, the case of Mr. A.L.W. As a boy, he wanted to become a mining engineer but his parents did not wish him to have a profession that might take him away from home. He is now, at twenty-four, an unhappy bookkeeper. He cannot afford to marry. That, too, might move him under another roof. The future stretches ahead and it is gray indeed.

You and I know that A.L.W. does not need to play the role he has come to accept, or stay in the drama in which he is acting so dubious a part. But is it not true of any of us that we could if we would change our role, and also dramatize a very different plot and action for our lives?

There are people who attribute their success in their human relations to the fact that they always carefully set the stage for each important interview or event. The situations they dealt with did not "just happen" when something came up. Let us admit that each and all of us should be happy-go-lucky in the ordinary and relaxed activities of our lives. Even a surgeon, or an experimenter designing atom bombs, has times of play and hours when a casual spontaneity is in order. But such men must set the stage in the important operations with which they deal.

It is not only wise to learn stage setting, but also the art of giving oneself stage direction and to develop roles for each activity of one's life. There is no better way to avoid strain or to achieve a poised success.

In my earlier years I had seven distinctly different forms of experience to which I had to adapt. First came my office practice as a consulting psychologist. Second, my activities as a constant lecturer. Thirdly, my work as a writer of books and articles. Fourthly, the adjustment essential to home life. Then there followed in due order the adaptation necessary to social contacts, commuting and traveling and the hours and hours in hotels all over the country. Countless are the people who said, "I should think such a strenuous life would wear you out." It would have had I not prepared myself for it. I avoided the strain by creating conduct patterns for each of the seven circumstances. In other words, I created some constructive roles, and so familiarized myself with the different parts I must play that there was no tension or further effort needed. The adjustments were automatic. Nor need there be anything unnatural, untrue or insincere in this procedure.

As in my case at least, each part I played was an adjustment of myself as a self to the functional activity. As a lecturer I was still myself: that is, myself while functioning as a lecturer. But, believe me, I was no longer a lecturer when I entered the door of my home. I changed my role completely, but I was still myself. Incidentally, I have known several lecturers who made no such practical adjustment. They were still lecturers when with their families—to everyone's dismay. I also know a few clinical psychologists who perpetually analyze their wives and children, to their ultimate destruction.

There is no wiser procedure than to dramatize an adjusted behavior pattern for the essential activities of one's life. The use of such a therapy is the seventh concrete step.

8 REHEARSAL PLANNING

*C*AN you not easily imagine how poor a presentation an actor might make if he had never rehearsed his part before he stepped onto the stage? Ellen Terry, one of the greatest Shakespearian actresses, used to sit alone in her room living in her mind every motion of how she would play a part. Not only did she picture her acting in advance and hear all the intonations in her voice, but she also created the mood of how she would feel when, for example, she would be on the stage playing in, let us say, *Macbeth*. She thought out and lived imaginatively every aspect of Lady Macbeth's thought, feeling and action. These conduct patterns she then actuated when in rehearsal.

Because of its long-established use in the theater, this method is often spoken of as *rehearsal thinking*. Without it every actor would do his work with desperate nervousness and a killing strain. It should also be remembered that rehearsing is not done in public. The actors are free of the responsibility of doing their work well enough to please ticket holders. Such a futile method is reserved for the way most people try to accomplish their desires in daily life.

By the use of rehearsal thinking, an actor concretely habituates a series of behavior patterns of the way he is later on to fulfill his part in a play. They then become spontaneous automatisms. He hears in his mind the way he will speak. He feels with deep emotion the way he will be stirred when the play is produced. Gradually the machinery of behavior that is his brain, his nerves, his glands and muscles becomes conditioned to certain ways of moving, looking and speaking. He has made a series of response patterns that have become well-cut engrams on the white matter of his brain, and they have thereby become definite designs. They are organized into a series of conduct patterns in his mind. When the play is produced, the actor has merely to release these well-organized motions of body, thought and feeling.

It is not yet clearly realized by most people that this rehearsal is just as important for anyone and everyone confronted with an important problem if he wishes to deal with it spontaneously and with ease. To have, for example, two querulous mothers in the home is a serious situation for any married couple. Jealousy and faultfinding are inevitable. Scenes as definite as those on any stage are unavoidable. Skill in handling them does not just happen without thought and planning. But they can be dealt with automatically and without strain by well-rehearsed patterns of advisable conduct and then applied with firmness.

In such a situation, if there is no trained consultant handy, one should sit down with some sympathetic intimate to consider the type of scenes that most commonly come to pass. Then if a series of behavior patterns is wisely conceived and

83

appropriate conversation prepared, three-quarters of the problem will disappear.

Nothing could be more silly than the thoughtless spouting to our associates that we too often indulge in when difficulties arise.

Alonzo Brice had three people in his life who constantly forced their opinions upon him: his partner, an elderly father and his militant daughter. Conversations with each of them about the things that concerned Alonzo and themselves were endless. For years Alonzo allowed these verbal battles to smother him. He acted in each case as if their arrival were a great surprise. A tension resulted, to such a degree that his doctor feared for his heart.

One day a scene took place in the little garden back of his house, to which Alonzo fled in retreat from his verbal enemies. On this occasion he became quiet, overcome not only by the barrage he had received from his vociferous daughter, but by the effect upon his aging body. After it was over he sat on a garden seat panting. He did not know that his Italian gardener, who came once a week to trim the shrubs and mow the lawn, had witnessed the entire scene.

Bashfully, but driven by concern for his employer, Artelio came up to him. "Why don't you-a mak-a da preparation . . . de plan-a what you-a say, what you-a do, so you not get-a shock and strain-a your heart?"

"What can I do, Artelio?" he panted. "She's a she-devil."

"Dat's-a all right, Mr. Brice. But da she-devil, she always speak-a da same way . . . ask-a for moneey. Any way you put it, you pay. Why not plan-a what-a you say, what-a you do, and not get excite. You get-a so work up you by and by kill yourself."

"You think I ought to plan beforehand. Is that it?"

"Sure. Every day or so these-a talks . . . same talks like in

84

what-a you call a play . . . leetle dramas. See? Now why you not rehearse-a your part? Is dat ze word—rehearse? Do-a and say-a what you are to do-a . . . to say-a. That make it ol' story so you not get-a excite."

Had the advice come from his doctor, Alonzo would have listened, then paid no attention to it, for that is the way most people do when they receive professional help. But to have it come from his gardener intrigued him. After all, Artelio, who was nearly eighty and still hale and hearty, must have some secret to allow him to live so long and so well.

"Thank you, Artelio," he said, rising. "I'll try your idea."

"Make-a you moch-a less strain." Artelio smiled with benign concern. Then, patting his employer as a mother might a child, he added with great firmness, "You live-a moch longer if you no get excite."

The advice functioned like magic, not at once but more and more successfully each time Alonzo had sat in his room and thought over the kind of affray he had so long had to endure with his daughter.

"Then why not prepare for my talks with my partner, and with Father?" he mused.

Elated by his success in establishing automatic response patterns, and amused that he now found the verbal battles with his three adversaries interesting and almost fun, Alonzo confided his experiences to his friend, Fulton, but was somewhat surprised at the hearty laughter his story produced.

"Last week," Fulton explained, as his mirth subsided, "I went to hear a lecture by a fellow who talks about things like that, and he explained how one could use what he called preliminary dialogue."

"What's that?" Alonzo asked.

"It's just what you're doing. Only this fellow said to use it for every conversation where one had to make effort. He was talking to a group of salesmen about preparing what one needed to say."

"Hm," Alonzo mused. "I think I'll even prepare for my wife's return from visiting her mother. It might make it easier."

Many a man's success has depended upon the making of preliminary dialogues. Many years ago, on an island in Italy, I spent three months talking to the trees in a lovely little woods. Sometimes I lectured to them for hours. Then I imagined a question period. Each tree had a different problem to present to me. Whatever success I had as a speaker in the years that followed I owe to this preliminary effort. The experience convinced me that, whenever one has an important interview ahead of him, he should familiarize himself not only with what he wisely may say, but also with what he should not say. Nor should one forget to imagine what the other person, or persons, is likely to say and to ask.

Preliminary dialogue is a form of psychic practice. I know of many people who not only use advanced effort in order to be more skillful in conversation but who have all sorts of private programs. They plan performances in their minds, seeing and feeling as well as hearing themselves in various activities. Some of them also decide what they will not do when various occasions arise.

Such psychic practice does not make one self-conscious. That is just what it eliminates, for behavior, once it is well rehearsed, becomes spontaneous and automatic. All skills give one confidence, and any and every sort of skill can be greatly increased by repetitively experiencing in one's mind the way he intends to behave later on. You surely realize how self-conscious you would feel if you tried to dance without knowing how. But do you realize that one learns to dance far better and much more easily, if he observes good dancing and then, in his mind, lives in the act of dancing?

86

You can correct mistakes more easily when visualized in your mind than in physical action. Practice mentally what you wish to do before you try to do it.

Rehearsal thinking as a form of mental practice is the eighth concrete step.

9 INDUCED AUTOSUGGESTION

*T*HERE could be no greater mistake than to believe that the knowledge we need to meet our problems must all of it be "modern." Great wisdoms were known in the past. The use of suggestion is one of these. It has played a part in the life and thought of man in every period of time and in each country of the earth. It has had an important place in the arts and sciences as well as in medicine and statecraft. In certain lands it was the controlling power in religion. It is a definite means of creating sensory equivalents and has therefore played a great part in the progress of man.

The ancients well understood that suggestion touches our deepest motive centers, and is a means not only of self-control but of command over others. In its positive form it is magnificent. In its negative aspects it is one of the most destructive of all the response patterns of the mind. This is because it creates injurious sensory equivalents: patterns of failure, sickness and disaster.

Especially is suggestion important because of its susceptibility to the influence of fear and the destruction of confidence. A person's imagination then becomes involved so that he may be as powerless at self-decision as a creature under the influence of hypnosis.

Literature fairly teems with descriptions of fear-ridden imagination. In *Hamlet,* we read: "And my imaginations are as foul as Vulcan's Smithy"; and after another fancied woe: "the big, round tears coursed one another down his innocent nose in piteous chase."

We know today that one of the most destructive tendencies in human life is the negativity of thought and feeling that results from the reception of fear-ridden suggestion. Nor is its power diminished when it is self-induced rather than caused by the malignant influence of another person. We know that its impressions on the mind are never good, that, as Cicero put it long ago, "fear is not a lasting teacher of duty"; that fear, as Emerson explained, "always springs from ignorance."

In this reference, Francis Bacon stated: "Nothing is to be feared but fear"; and as Balzac explained: "After all, our worst misfortunes never happen and most miseries be in anticipation." These we must learn to control, and in many instances to ignore, or our relation to life can never become easy. "He has not learned the lesson of life who does not every day surmount a fear," wrote the wise Emerson.

Realizing as one must the tremendous power of negative autosuggestion, and the devastation it can create in all parts of a person's organism, I would be the last to ignore its positive efficiency as a means of creating constructive equivalents of mental health and sound achievement, for in and of itself it is not evil.

I would also be the last person to assert that all the great accomplishers necessarily found imagery the only suitable technique. Even if most people respond better to visual than to auditory processes, it is yet true that some natures gain surer results when emphasis is put on a verbal design rather than on one that depends upon a visual method.

The ideal technique is, of course, a multiple activity wherein a number of helpful methods are merged into one dynamic equivalent of the result desired. But it is not wise to depend upon such a union until one is familiar with the separate procedures. At the same time, let us say again that distinctly auditory people achieve better results by the use of sound, and even of the written as well as the spoken word. For this reason induced autosuggestion should always be considered and used whenever possible.

This method is most definite in its structure. There are, let us assume, some difficult problems in your life. You may not be perfectly well or entirely free of emotional and mental aberrations. Self-consciousness, hypersensitivity, a feeling of frustration, times of depression, personal limitations may enter to hinder your success in daily efforts. To overcome these causes of misfortune, and to strengthen your handling of the circumstances with which you must deal, autosuggestion has proved a mighty tool. The word *induced* is added to describe the fact that it is not a *general* autosuggestion that you use, but one specifically constructed to deal with each important problem in your life.

In other words, this method differs from simple autosuggestion in that each time it is used a single idea (with thought, feeling and action) is chosen to create the designs of conduct that will bring a precise purpose to pass. Emile Coué developed the term and used the method to cure various diseases. A man who could not raise his right arm because of functional paralysis was taught to say, "I shall. My arm will raise above my head." When by himself he said this many times until the arm-raising pattern was cut in his mind. He then succeeded.

Such a statement is concrete. It is a verbal means of projecting patterns of constructive conduct into one's mind so that they then function automatically.

This therapy acts on the engrams of the brain that have been conditioned by speech. It reconditions them. From infancy on, most of us have been given many suggestions; but usually in negative form. "You can't," "You mustn't," "You shouldn't," "It's wrong," "It's no use." Countless failure impressions have been established that associate so automatically with the stimulus of various situations that the "can't" suggestion makes the negative become a fact. The "It's no use" suggestion *makes* it no use. The evil impression comes into control. Induced autosuggestion, by creating new and powerful equivalents of good activity, breaks up these imprisoning thoughts.

Unless as adults we use a reconditioning therapy, the impressions made on us in the past can cause behavior that creates equivalents of constant failure or personal and social discomfort. Autosuggestion is an essential means of releasing the person's mind from the masses of verbal conditioning that might otherwise distort him for life and make the development of good habit paths most difficult.

Not until a person learns to hate intellectual cynicism and sophisticated skepticism, and to understand the value of hope, the power of belief and the importance of faith, are any therapies fully efficacious, autosuggestion least of all. Coué accomplished much with the warmhearted French peasants who came to him, and very little with the smart, hurried Americans who doubted his method. Jesus cured thousands by his therapies, but not the Pharisees. As with the use of visual imagery, a person must have belief in autosuggestion. His emotions must be touched. He must *feel* the way of life that is suggested, and live in the action that is being impressed upon his mind. No therapy is of value to anyone who does not surrender himself to that therapy.

It is for this reason that faith is essential to the success of this technique, a faith fully equal to that which a person has given to his belief in what he fears. One needs just such a faith as Jesus in every case demanded before he would attempt to heal.

"Faith is the force of life," wrote Tolstoy, but he did not know why. Oliver Wendell Holmes tells us it is because "Faith always implies a disbelief in the lesser facts in favor of the greater." It is a trust then that causes a person to discard the negative suggestion he has received and supplant it with a positive one. He then surrenders his thought and emotion to the greater and more constructive values.

In any case we know today that no truer words were ever penned than those of Boiste: "He who has lost confidence can lose nothing more." But on the positive side we know that he who by the use of constructive techniques has mastered the ways of conquest gains more than confidence in *himself*. A *new* power comes to pass that is greater than any self-engendered belief. A confidence in what purposeful designs can do for him is a faith that so far surpasses a trust in his own ego that the two can never be compared. While it is true, as Cicero said, that a man's courage is full of faith, it is equally true that a man's faith is full of courage. Nor is there any strength greater than that which is fortified by the dynamics we have been discussing.

Suggestion takes effect more fully when one is alone and quiet. The response is singularly powerful if used just before going to sleep or just as one awakens in the morning.

In our American life we need more time for meditation. We marvel at some of the achievements of the Hindus without realizing that they are made possible by the Oriental habit of quiet. A sense of leisure is an important factor in the use of any therapy. Thus when you attempt to use this technique of autosuggestion give yourself time. The human mind cannot be successfully hurried.

Unlike the image-making process, you can use autosuggestion even while you are in action and making effort to accomplish a needed task. There is an innate impulse to use it in this way. Have you not heard people talking to themselves in some emergency or when endeavoring to accomplish a hard piece of work? Many times while in action I have said to myself, "Hold on now, Davie, no strain. Don't put on too much steam. Slow down. Take it easy. Remember, old boy, don't push." This is good therapy, and it works.

Let us consider the case of a man we will call Ralph Stoneham, a man who is now a successful manufacturer in an Eastern city. His father had known William James, and he had had the good fortune to hear about autosuggestion in his youth. It did not seem to him, as it does to some people, to be a self-conscious procedure, but just good sense. Because of this faith in the method, he used it to create equivalents of his desires in all the major activities of his life.

There was a time when as a boy he got into all sorts of trouble because of a hot temper. By manhood, by the use of autosuggestion, he had put what he called a "check valve" on his explosive tendency, telling himself quietly how a mature and thoughtful person would behave. He repetitively stated that just such behavior would be his own.

Ralph had originally had trouble meeting strangers, and often when suddenly confronted with having to make an introduction he stuttered badly. Determined to get rid of a handicap that would seriously hamper his career, Ralph talked to himself about what the sensory equivalents of relaxed conduct would be in any such situation. He taught himself to feel

93

at ease. "There's nothing to fear from a stranger," he repeatedly told himself. "I shall remain in a comfortable frame of mind. My nerves will not become tense. My mind will not be locked in anxiety. I shall have no closure of my thought. I shall not stutter. There is no need of this tension. I shall act as one does when at ease. I shall *feel* at ease."

Ralph created in his mind a series of dramatic equivalents of typical activities in his life: seeing, hearing and sensing how he would play his part in the kind of events he would be likely to have in his business and personal life.

By the time he came to the "marriage years" he had eliminated the fear of girls that had constricted his spontaneity in boyhood. Nor were there any remnants of the embarrassment he had felt with younger children. In consequence he had no strain when his own offspring came along, and also no ill-at-easeness in the activities of intimacy. He had such good action patterns for his major experiences that he functioned inside of them with nonchalance.

Ralph in his earlier years had always dreaded to take business trips. This fear had greatly retarded his effort to gain the executive position he ultimately secured. The activity had entailed three factors that were at that time disturbing to him. First of all came the selling part of it. He had found it hard. He was so ill at ease that his customer was also uncomfortable.

He applied induced autosuggestion to his problem with satisfactory results. He gathered all the information he could as to what comradely communication and pleasant at-easeness were like. Then he had sales conversations with himself in his hotel room. Soon he felt such a sense of assurance that even in the presence of a resistant customer he was no longer a victim of nerves. "This is the stuff," he murmured, looking over the statement of his increased sales. "I can do it. This is the way for me."

With less exhaustion after a day of interviews he slept better. This added to his confidence until, like a snowball, he felt himself gathering power.

Ralph, however, did not stop there. He described to himself the situation he had to deal with when forced to travel at night. The pullmans were comfortable, but he had not slept well in them. It occurred to him to dramatize the sensory equivalents of good sleep in night travel. "The motion of the train after this," he asserted, "will rock me as if I were a baby in a cradle." And it did. "The tap, tap, tap of the rails will hereafter be a song to lull me to sleep." And so it became. "I can always ring for the porter when I need him. I am singularly safe, yet alone and free from bothers. Now I can relax completely." And that is what he learned to do.

Induced autosuggestion has been used successfully for countless forms of conquest when the equivalents of constructive action are clearly created. Men have won sweethearts by changes in their wooing that transformed them from stiff swains into ardent lovers. Later on in marriage the many unfamiliar requirements of intimacy have been turned from obstacles into happy victories, when the sensory equivalents that the induced suggestion created were definite. Women, unused to housework, have used induced autosuggestion to help them more swiftly to accomplish the details of domestic routine. Parent problems disappear when one is willing to train himself by well-chosen words for adjusting to children.

Since this technique is not limited to a special form, some people like to be by themselves and talk their suggestions out loud. Others prefer to induce the method silently, but quite as definitely as one does when he vocally concentrates on some special type of action. The method need not even be limited to conversational form. Some natures achieve better sensory equivalents if a written procedure is followed.

William James, a master of this technique quite as much as that of image-making, used to advise one to take two pieces

95

of typewriter paper, marking one negative, the other positive. He recommended that we deal with a single difficulty at a time whether or not it concerned our personal conduct or a situation external to ourselves. On the negative sheet he told us to write a descriptive equivalent of how we had in some way behaved badly that day: a confession of what we did in some situation we had found difficult. "Do not spare yourself," he said. "Describe fully, almost mercilessly, the mistakes you made, the tension you had, the strain you felt, the confusion that blocked the free use of your ability."

"Then," he suggested, "on the sheet marked *positive*, write out fully just how you feel a person with confidence and poise would have behaved. Describe his thoughtfulness and practicality in dealing with the situation. Take time to portray fully how the problem could be overcome." (This was, of course, a constructive sensory equivalent.) "Turn to the negative sheet on which you have written your confession of inadequacy. Read it over. Hate it. Repudiate it. Say to yourself, 'I'm getting over that sort of conduct.' Feel your revulsion so strongly that you take that sheet of paper, with its maudlin statements, and tear it to shreds. Fling it into the wastepaper basket. Now take the sheet that describes how the situation could have been constructively met. Read it carefully, and as you do so, *feel* yourself doing it that way with increasing power. Say to yourself, 'I shall do more and more this way.' "

These are not his exact words, as such statements, as far as I know, were never written by James. They are, however, an adequate phrasing of the ideas he verbally gave to some of us and that he so valued in his own personal experience. This advice came to us in conversations we shall never forget.

This practical means of self-direction is the ninth concrete step, each one of which is a more advanced form of a single therapy.

10 YOUR RESPONSE TO SUGGESTION

ONE of the most remarkable aspects of the human mind, and of the so-called "unconscious" levels of the mind, is its susceptibility to suggestion. Even when we are to some degree aware of it, and partially resent our tendency to be influenced, we are still often affected by what is said to us.

The story is told of a village loafer who went from one place to another about his little town to find some companionship to ease his idleness. Some of those who were tired of his perpetual presence decided to play a trick on him. They agreed to tell him on a certain morning how sick he looked. First the postmaster asked, "Feeling pretty bad today?"

"Why, no," responded the victim, "I'm all right."

"You look sick to me," the postmaster insisted. "Maybe you aren't so bad now, but you will be if you don't look out."

Somewhat upset at this promise of illness, the loafer ambled to the hardware store.

"Golly, what's happened to you?" the storekeeper cried.

"Well, I—" The man hesitated, recalling the postmaster's words. "I guess maybe I'm coming down with something."

Everywhere he went on his regular rounds, he received some sort of suggestion that portended illness or its imminent approach. By two o'clock he took to his bed. The doctor was called. Uninformed of the campaign that was on foot, he found his patient in a high fever. Believing that the man's system was clogged, he gave him castor oil; and how that added to the suggestion of imminent disease you can well imagine.

This is a true story of a certain village in the state of Maine, a part of the world full of natural psychologists and men with a certain rugged sense of humor. The experience may have been a little tough on the town loafer, but it was good for him. Its moral is good for us all, for none of us is entirely immune to suggestion.

NEGATIVE HETEROSUGGESTION APPROXIMATOR

One of the best ways to free yourself from strain is to check on the negative suggestions that people make to you. Perhaps you will be amazed to discover how often you are influenced, quite unconsciously, by destructive heterosuggestion. We all suffered from it in a most serious way in childhood and in our teens. Parents, uncles, aunts, neighbors, friends, teachers, playmates, all joined in a campaign of negative suggestions. But this depressing, failure-making process did not stop with one's majority, and few of us ever came of age in the opinion of our familial monitors.

As you study the following list, quietly affirm to yourself, "I shall not let myself be emotionally influenced by this kind of verbal barrage." If you are willing carefully to investigate this matter of heterosuggestion you will discover that many of the things said to you are in the form of propaganda. They are said to influence you and often to control you. This verbal maneuvering goes on all the time in every home, neighborhood, office, factory and club. It is not that people lie exactly, but they do color the truth so as to make you think, feel and act as they want you to, and in ways that are to their advantage.

Mark the following phrases, from zero to ten, to estimate the amount you feel you hear such remarks, or others about like them, from your associates, and are perhaps quite unconsciously influenced by them.

1. You are too enthusiastic   0 1 2 3 4 5 6 7 8 9 10
2. This is not the time to do it   0 1 2 3 4 5 6 7 8 9 10
3. You had better stay at home   0 1 2 3 4 5 6 7 8 9 10
4. There are so many accidents   0 1 2 3 4 5 6 7 8 9 10
5. Most marriages end in divorce   0 1 2 3 4 5 6 7 8 9 10
6. Pretty soon you'll be bankrupt   0 1 2 3 4 5 6 7 8 9 10
7. There's no use taking such a risk   0 1 2 3 4 5 6 7 8 9 10
8. Let's look the obstacles in the face   0 1 2 3 4 5 6 7 8 9 10
9. It's altogether too difficult   0 1 2 3 4 5 6 7 8 9 10
10. Somebody has to say no   0 1 2 3 4 5 6 7 8 9 10
11. You cause me lots of worry   0 1 2 3 4 5 6 7 8 9 10
12. You should not be so confident   0 1 2 3 4 5 6 7 8 9 10
13. Who do you think you are?   0 1 2 3 4 5 6 7 8 9 10
14. You aren't strong enough to stand it   0 1 2 3 4 5 6 7 8 9 10
15. You look pretty poorly   0 1 2 3 4 5 6 7 8 9 10
16. Your nerves are all on edge   0 1 2 3 4 5 6 7 8 9 10

17. Germs are everywhere
    nowadays   0 1 2 3 4 5 6 7 8 9 10
18. You never seem to con-
    sider the dangers   0 1 2 3 4 5 6 7 8 9 10
19. It's so easy to lose
    money   0 1 2 3 4 5 6 7 8 9 10
20. You get so excited
    about it   0 1 2 3 4 5 6 7 8 9 10
21. Someone must hold
    you down   0 1 2 3 4 5 6 7 8 9 10
22. I doubt if you can put
    it over   0 1 2 3 4 5 6 7 8 9 10
23. Failure would be such
    a disgrace   0 1 2 3 4 5 6 7 8 9 10
24. You expect too much
    of love   0 1 2 3 4 5 6 7 8 9 10
25. All you make is ex-
    cuses   0 1 2 3 4 5 6 7 8 9 10
26. It's time you grew up 0 1 2 3 4 5 6 7 8 9 10
27. How can you be so
    stupid?   0 1 2 3 4 5 6 7 8 9 10
28. Helping you is a thank-
    less task   0 1 2 3 4 5 6 7 8 9 10
29. You'll be sorry some
    day   0 1 2 3 4 5 6 7 8 9 10
30. What will people
    think?   0 1 2 3 4 5 6 7 8 9 10
31. You aren't free to do
    what you choose   0 1 2 3 4 5 6 7 8 9 10
32. Nobody else would do
    it   0 1 2 3 4 5 6 7 8 9 10
33. Why are you so stub-
    born?   0 1 2 3 4 5 6 7 8 9 10
34. I never heard of any-
    thing so foolish   0 1 2 3 4 5 6 7 8 9 10
35. You couldn't make a
    greater mistake   0 1 2 3 4 5 6 7 8 9 10

36.	I think you are un-teachable	o	1	2	3	4	5	6	7	8	9	10
37.	So you're superior to reason	o	1	2	3	4	5	6	7	8	9	10
38.	I don't like your associates	o	1	2	3	4	5	6	7	8	9	10
39.	You think the sky is the limit	o	1	2	3	4	5	6	7	8	9	10
40.	You make me ashamed of you	o	1	2	3	4	5	6	7	8	9	10
41.	You don't respect authority	o	1	2	3	4	5	6	7	8	9	10
42.	I'm only trying to save you	o	1	2	3	4	5	6	7	8	9	10
43.	I never saw such complacency	o	1	2	3	4	5	6	7	8	9	10
44.	You really aren't qualified	o	1	2	3	4	5	6	7	8	9	10
45.	People won't like you if you do that	o	1	2	3	4	5	6	7	8	9	10
46.	You always think only of yourself	o	1	2	3	4	5	6	7	8	9	10
47.	You can't trust anyone nowadays	o	1	2	3	4	5	6	7	8	9	10
48.	You haven't had enough experience	o	1	2	3	4	5	6	7	8	9	10
49.	Don't you care about your reputation?	o	1	2	3	4	5	6	7	8	9	10
50.	You should want to do your duty	o	1	2	3	4	5	6	7	8	9	10

A score of nearly 500 means that you are devastatingly affected by what people say to you. This is the key to poor health and failure in life. A score of about 400 shows that your response to heterosuggestion is still a serious matter, and a score of around 300 reveals the fact you are still injured by what people say. If your score is 200 or less, you are doing fairly well in maintaining independence of thought, but if it is only 100—well, ask your friends if they agree that you are so free of negative influence.

NEGATIVE AUTOSUGGESTION APPROXIMATOR

Another of the valuable ways to free yourself from strain is to check on your habit of negative autosuggestion. You may not use any of the phrases in the following list, but I am sure you know people who do. You can trace their failures, unhappiness and ill health to such negative suggestion, can you not? Every effect has a cause, and one of the most prevalent causes of sickness, misery and despair is to be found in the repetitive use of such destructive verbalism.

Mark the phrases from zero to ten to measure the amount or number of times you think or use such a phrase, or even a similar one. The language does not have to be exact, it is the idea, the spirit, of this kind of remark we are trying to measure, in order to estimate how much negative autosuggestion is in control of unconscious thought.

1. Nothing good ever happens to me   0 1 2 3 4 5 6 7 8 9 10
2. It'll never work   0 1 2 3 4 5 6 7 8 9 10
3. The world's sure going to the dogs   0 1 2 3 4 5 6 7 8 9 10
4. I might as well be dead   0 1 2 3 4 5 6 7 8 9 10
5. What's the use, nobody cares   0 1 2 3 4 5 6 7 8 9 10
6. I know I can't do it   0 1 2 3 4 5 6 7 8 9 10
7. I might as well give up   0 1 2 3 4 5 6 7 8 9 10
8. I never feel good in the morning   0 1 2 3 4 5 6 7 8 9 10
9. Nothing ever works for me   0 1 2 3 4 5 6 7 8 9 10

10.	I don't expect much of marriage	0	1	2	3	4	5	6	7	8	9	10
11.	I never have any luck	0	1	2	3	4	5	6	7	8	9	10
12.	I'm afraid it won't come out well	0	1	2	3	4	5	6	7	8	9	10
13.	I don't find much generosity	0	1	2	3	4	5	6	7	8	9	10
14.	I prefer dogs to people	0	1	2	3	4	5	6	7	8	9	10
15.	Romance doesn't last long	0	1	2	3	4	5	6	7	8	9	10
16.	Love? Don't make me laugh	0	1	2	3	4	5	6	7	8	9	10
17.	Happiness is not for me	0	1	2	3	4	5	6	7	8	9	10
18.	It's no use trying so hard	0	1	2	3	4	5	6	7	8	9	10
19.	No one will thank me for it	0	1	2	3	4	5	6	7	8	9	10
20.	Gratitude is something I never get	0	1	2	3	4	5	6	7	8	9	10
21.	All I do is worry	0	1	2	3	4	5	6	7	8	9	10
22.	They can't sell me that stuff	0	1	2	3	4	5	6	7	8	9	10
23.	I am always misunderstood	0	1	2	3	4	5	6	7	8	9	10
24.	I can never do as I want to	0	1	2	3	4	5	6	7	8	9	10
25.	I am too old to start anything new	0	1	2	3	4	5	6	7	8	9	10
26.	Faith is too sentimental for me	0	1	2	3	4	5	6	7	8	9	10
27.	It's all so discouraging	0	1	2	3	4	5	6	7	8	9	10
28.	I hate that kind of thing	0	1	2	3	4	5	6	7	8	9	10
29.	Trouble never comes to an end	0	1	2	3	4	5	6	7	8	9	10

30.	God never helps me	0	1	2	3	4	5	6	7	8	9	10
31.	Life is nothing but compromise	0	1	2	3	4	5	6	7	8	9	10
32.	Things become worse and worse	0	1	2	3	4	5	6	7	8	9	10
33.	I'm blamed for all I do	0	1	2	3	4	5	6	7	8	9	10
34.	Life is an endless grind	0	1	2	3	4	5	6	7	8	9	10
35.	All I have is struggle	0	1	2	3	4	5	6	7	8	9	10
36.	Love is an empty dream	0	1	2	3	4	5	6	7	8	9	10
37.	It's little that I get out of it	0	1	2	3	4	5	6	7	8	9	10
38.	I have no future worth having	0	1	2	3	4	5	6	7	8	9	10
39.	It is fools who have hope	0	1	2	3	4	5	6	7	8	9	10
40.	It's easy to make promises	0	1	2	3	4	5	6	7	8	9	10
41.	This place is just a dump	0	1	2	3	4	5	6	7	8	9	10
42.	And everything is heaped on me	0	1	2	3	4	5	6	7	8	9	10
43.	I'm more worn out every day	0	1	2	3	4	5	6	7	8	9	10
44.	Life isn't worth the effort	0	1	2	3	4	5	6	7	8	9	10
45.	You just can't win	0	1	2	3	4	5	6	7	8	9	10
46.	I've quit trying	0	1	2	3	4	5	6	7	8	9	10
47.	I never get a break	0	1	2	3	4	5	6	7	8	9	10
48.	We grow more old and decrepit	0	1	2	3	4	5	6	7	8	9	10
49.	There isn't ever time enough	0	1	2	3	4	5	6	7	8	9	10
50.	Who really cares anyway?	0	1	2	3	4	5	6	7	8	9	10

A score of nearly 500 reveals the fact that you make yourself fail, create your unhappiness and suggest the sicknesses that come upon you. If perhaps you also had a high score in the heterosuggestion test, then God pity you. You need professional help. A score of about 400 shows that you persistently tear yourself down and constrict your life, and a score of around 300 tells us that negativity is a destructive tendency in your life. Even a score of 200 or more shows you are not free of dubious pessimism. If your score is 100 or less, you have a fairly good affirmative attitude, and if it is only 50, you must be radiantly happy, exceptionally well and conspicuously successful.

CONSTRUCTIVE AUTOSUGGESTION APPROXIMATOR

How often do you strengthen your morale by positive affirmation? Have you formed the habit of consciously building up your powers of conquest and endurance? Have you established a good and logical expectancy pattern? If not, here is one of the best of all rules to follow. Observe that people who live under the weight of anxiety, people who worry until their health is injured, people who are unhappy and fail in life, have a habit of matching every constructive attitude with a destructive one. Whenever a good thing happens or someone speaks encouragingly, they bring up a fear pattern, a thought of danger or dread to balance it. In other words, they submerge every positive value with a negative one.

To succeed, to maintain health, to be happy, reverse this evil process. Instead, refuse to accept any and every negative until you have matched it with a typical positive.

It is the good that overcomes the evil, the constructive course of action that conquers the destructive trends. Insist also on developing as a general attitude a positive frame of mind. To discover whether or not you are already doing so, fill out the following test.

Mark the phrases from zero to ten to measure the amount or number of times you make such affirmative suggestions to yourself. The language does not have to be the same, only somewhat similar. It is the idea, the spirit, of affirmation we are striving to measure, to see how well you have learned to live your life constructively.

1.	I shall think before I act	0 1 2 3 4 5 6 7 8 9 10
2.	I shall strive to establish good plans	0 1 2 3 4 5 6 7 8 9 10
3.	I shall not worry about results	0 1 2 3 4 5 6 7 8 9 10
4.	I shall not resist problems	0 1 2 3 4 5 6 7 8 9 10
5.	I intend to win	0 1 2 3 4 5 6 7 8 9 10
6.	Things will be better by and by	0 1 2 3 4 5 6 7 8 9 10
7.	There is always to-morrow	0 1 2 3 4 5 6 7 8 9 10
8.	No one can do better than his best	0 1 2 3 4 5 6 7 8 9 10
9.	Nature helps us if we let her	0 1 2 3 4 5 6 7 8 9 10
10.	It's always darkest before daylight	0 1 2 3 4 5 6 7 8 9 10
11.	Most troubles pass away	0 1 2 3 4 5 6 7 8 9 10
12.	I will use logic in planning my work, then use thought in working my plan	0 1 2 3 4 5 6 7 8 9 10

13. I will value my integrity above my worldly honors 0 1 2 3 4 5 6 7 8 9 10

14. I shall try to keep an open mind 0 1 2 3 4 5 6 7 8 9 10

15. I shall examine my prejudices 0 1 2 3 4 5 6 7 8 9 10

16. I shall seek a way of life that expresses the true "me" 0 1 2 3 4 5 6 7 8 9 10

17. I shall look for the good in everything and relate to it 0 1 2 3 4 5 6 7 8 9 10

18. I will not identify myself with negative remarks or accusations 0 1 2 3 4 5 6 7 8 9 10

19. I will at all times be sincere 0 1 2 3 4 5 6 7 8 9 10

20. I shall always remember that "life is for growth" 0 1 2 3 4 5 6 7 8 9 10

21. Every experience contains some benefit, and I shall look for it 0 1 2 3 4 5 6 7 8 9 10

22. I shall be honest with myself as well as with others 0 1 2 3 4 5 6 7 8 9 10

23. I will think of myself as maturing, not growing old 0 1 2 3 4 5 6 7 8 9 10

24. I shall visualize myself as a success and strive toward it 0 1 2 3 4 5 6 7 8 9 10

25. I shall keep a sense of humor 0 1 2 3 4 5 6 7 8 9 10

26. I will maintain enthusi-
    asm and a zest for life 0 1 2 3 4 5 6 7 8 9 10
27. I will do my best in
    every situation or task,
    and then "let go" 0 1 2 3 4 5 6 7 8 9 10
28. I will not allow nega-
    tive thought to control
    me 0 1 2 3 4 5 6 7 8 9 10
29. I will look for the good
    and overlook the short-
    comings in others 0 1 2 3 4 5 6 7 8 9 10
30. I will look for some-
    thing interesting in
    every task required of
    me 0 1 2 3 4 5 6 7 8 9 10
31. I will balance my bless-
    ings against my disap-
    pointments 0 1 2 3 4 5 6 7 8 9 10
32. I will guard my
    thoughts, knowing that
    "what I concentrate on
    I attract" 0 1 2 3 4 5 6 7 8 9 10
33. I shall adjust and
    reconcile, not compro-
    mise 0 1 2 3 4 5 6 7 8 9 10
34. Courageous daring is
    my motto 0 1 2 3 4 5 6 7 8 9 10
35. My choices shall be
    validated 0 1 2 3 4 5 6 7 8 9 10
36. I shall not be dogmatic 0 1 2 3 4 5 6 7 8 9 10
37. Let me avoid all ex-
    treme conclusions 0 1 2 3 4 5 6 7 8 9 10
38. Especially let me be-
    come alert and aware 0 1 2 3 4 5 6 7 8 9 10
39. I shall develop forti-
    tude 0 1 2 3 4 5 6 7 8 9 10

40.	Let me never cease to initiate	0	1	2	3	4	5	6	7	8	9	10
41.	Of all experience I shall find the causes	0	1	2	3	4	5	6	7	8	9	10
42.	Never shall I become lost in effects	0	1	2	3	4	5	6	7	8	9	10
43.	I shall keep my margin with courtesy	0	1	2	3	4	5	6	7	8	9	10
44.	Let me be diligent but never toilsome	0	1	2	3	4	5	6	7	8	9	10
45.	I shall maintain a serene persistence	0	1	2	3	4	5	6	7	8	9	10
46.	Let me follow my aspirations	0	1	2	3	4	5	6	7	8	9	10
47.	I shall execute my purposes	0	1	2	3	4	5	6	7	8	9	10
48.	Let me never become smug or priggish	0	1	2	3	4	5	6	7	8	9	10
49.	I shall seek the inner meanings of experience	0	1	2	3	4	5	6	7	8	9	10
50.	What is congenial shall be my choice	0	1	2	3	4	5	6	7	8	9	10

A score of nearly 500 means that you possess a magnificently constructive frame of mind and can accomplish miracles. A score of about 400 still implies an unusual poise and perception. If the score is as high as 300, you are still well above average in positive thinking. Over 200 is, or should be, about normal in affirmative insight, while if your score is only 100, you are slipping from constructive perception. A score as low as 50 tells us why your life is as it is, with too little health and happiness. It also suggests that you see your doctor as soon as possible.

Estimating out your response to suggestion is the tenth step in the art of successful living.

11 THE ACTUATION PROCESS

*P*ERHAPS no single instrument of enjoyment has ever swept the civilized world as suddenly as television. Combining as it does visual and auditory processes in the familiar environment of the home, it reaches more directly into human consciousness than any device man has so far created. For this reason it is a most perfect symbol of image-making and autosuggestion, merged as one dynamic means to invincible living. But it is more than this, for a fourth great technique comes into being in television—that of expression. Without the portrayal of thought and emotion through action, television would lose its dynamic power. Herein is a mighty key to the full art of living.

What you are witnessing on your television screen is an example of the way you should unite the visual and auditory aspects of thought and emotion, thereby creating fuller equivalents of what you desire to develop in your life. Upon this procedure, as it was repetitively applied to the world's work, the development of civilization depended.

To Thomas Carlyle this dynamic way of living was a veritable creed. He wrote: "The latest gospel in this world is: know thy work and do it." He was aware of how few people use such constructive ways of living. They read such admonitions and say to themselves, "Of course." "Why, yes, that is so obvious." It all seems so simple they do little to put it into operation.

Matthew Arnold described the failure of such behavior very perfectly: "Most men eddy about here and there." While the wise Confucius tells us: "If a man take no thought of what is distant, he will find sorrow near at hand."

There is nothing stranger, however, than the way such great thinkers applied the truths they wrote about in some one area of life, and failed to use it where in their own special case it was most needed. Consider, for example, the life of Samuel Coleridge. No one ever lectured better on a philosophic adjustment to life. No one ever so tragically failed to apply it as a means of establishing a competent work habit. "A man without forethought scarcely deserves the name of a man," he once wrote, and went on lengthily to say that a man was otherwise little more than a beast.

Yet Coleridge, who was said to have had one of the greatest minds England ever produced, not only twiddled away most of his life, but allowed a drug habit to ruin it. His forethought was indeed far from the efficient and crisp self-command of Wellington, who wrote of his preparation for the battle of Waterloo: "There is no mistake; there has been no mistake, and there shall be no mistake."

Coleridge failed as many others have done because he did not embody his plans and philosophic concepts in a concrete manner. It was left as fantasy and affirmation—good theory without practice.

How can we be sure that we so firmly establish the designs for what we desire to achieve that they enduringly remain? By what means is the visual imagery and the autosuggestion we use turned into active sensory equivalents? We do not wish to remind ourselves constantly to use these great therapies. We want them to function of their own accord. The effort we make to establish them must be an effort to reduce effort or it is not truly valuable. To accomplish this result repetitive embodiment in physical expression is an important step in the habituating of any such therapies.

We must first, however, fully consider why this is so and sufficiently emphasize what doing does to the doer. In co-operation with Lange, William James developed what is called the James-Lange theory of the affect of the body on the mind. It teaches that we are as much affected mentally and emotionally by the way our bodies behave as our bodies are affected by our thoughts and feelings.

James believed that if you sit in a slumped position you will soon feel sad; if you weep you will feel sadder. In other words, the positions, poses and behavior of our bodies affect our minds, and cause sensations in the nervous system that are good or bad according to the type of physical stimulus that creates them. In the latter part of his life James modified the original theory, believing that the bodily processes did not start our moods but definitely intensified them.

Happiness or sadness, comfort or anxiety, in our thoughts and feelings instigate our frames of mind, which are soon reflected in our physical behavior. If we surrender to this negative trend, the bodily disfunctions increase our maladjustment. If, on the other hand, we refuse to allow our moods to control our physical activities, much of the mental aberration is eliminated. Out of this early teaching came what is now called the *actuation process*.

It is an interesting fact that the easiest people to help by the means of modern psychotherapies are actors and actresses. They are used to playing a part: sincerely portraying moods and mental attitudes. They know that acting need not be dissimulation. They have been trained to recognize the relation between bodily expression and the inner actions that motivate conduct. For this reason they respond well to the actuation process as a means of creating and stabilizing the purposive designs of the ways they wish to live.

This method is not hard to understand. It consists in persistently behaving in given situations in the way you believe a poised, alert and confident person would behave, and continuing to act in this manner *no matter how you temporarily feel*. It is built on the conclusion that if you continue to function in a constructive way, your brain centers, nerves, glands and viscera will become affected by the physical demonstration, and after a while your thoughts and feelings will be pulled out of their negative state. You then become impelled to go with the sensory equivalents of that constructive conduct that you have created by mental imagery and autosuggestion. The actuation process also posits the realization that fine behavior patterns can be created through which your later thoughts and feelings easily flow. You thereby make the changes permanent.

This therapy depends for its efficacy on the way habits are formed. We start doing something in a certain manner and quite unconsciously identify ourselves with that kind of doing. By this act we give power to the process and come to feel that such conduct belongs to us.

The fact is that our brain centers, nerves, glands and viscera have become conditioned by repetitive action until that way of doing is embedded in our organisms. Actuation then is a method of creating training patterns until they become sensory equivalents that are so habituated that they act thereafter of themselves.

In whatever way you behave, emotion is aroused. This feeling is then connected with that particular type of action. The emotion by its motive power (its e-motion) then impels the repetitive action and makes it continue until it becomes a functioning pattern of the organism.

It has not been clearly recognized even by psychologists that emotion is the key to habit. Is it not the emotional sensation that creates such bad habits as the abuse of alcohol and drugs, sexual delinquency and even over-eating? If something in your environment constantly frightens you and you continually cringe in fear, your sense of dread becomes established in your nervous system. On the other hand, if you refuse to exhibit the outer behavior of terror, face your fear squarely and maintain the pose you would have at a time of courage, the feeling of anxiety is diminished and no habit is formed. So with every fundamental gesture. Since behavior intensifies the type of thought and feeling that would characteristically produce that kind of behavior, the actuation process becomes a constructive means of entrenching good sensory equivalents and for avoiding the injurious forms of imagery and suggestion.

"Nothing is until it is ultimated," wrote Swedenborg. Actuation ultimates the constructive imagery. Positive types of suggestions then create action patterns in agreement with the good visual design. These are the architects. Actuation is the builder. One may haltingly attempt a subjective therapy for a while, such as imagery. Actuation, if used, gives it nerve structure and so embodies it that its influence is continuous.

There are some people who think they find it difficult to use the mental therapies we have so far discussed because such methods are carried on in the mind. They like to use processes

114

that are objectified into immediate action so that they can see themselves carrying out some new and better conduct. The actuation process possesses just this quality.

There are also those who, when suddenly confronted with some difficult situation, need to use a method which makes it possible for them to assert and control the way they wish to behave. Faced with emergencies, actuation is a blessing for them, for it permits them to experiment so as to find and apply the right psychic practice until their actions are perfected.

In the use of actuation, time is often of the essence, for by this means swift and sure adjustments can be made for the immediate issues in one's day. But let us not forget that by its use one does not successfully change the great trends, the more entrenched habits or overcome the more serious neurotic states. This cannot be done by actuation alone. Mental imagery and autosuggestion must have created constructive sensory equivalents, which precede it before it is applied in cases where serious abnormalities exist. One can, however, use actuation successfully for the time being and in any situation even if one's conduct is only an imitation of the way he knows a calm and self-disciplined person would behave.

It is in the expressions, the motions, the comings and goings, the doings and sayings of life that you can best apply this method. Experience, as we have already said, is a stage and you are one of the players. Events are part of a drama, and we all are impelled in any and all cases by an impulse to play a role. It should be a role that is true to ourselves, and not a part forced upon us by those who live in our social masquerade.

To help explain this procedure of actuation, William James wrote: "Action seems to follow feeling, but really action and feeling go together, and by regulating the action, which is under the more direct control of the will, we can indirectly regulate the feeling which is not."

The actuation process is obviously the most concrete of the therapies. Even though it does not have permanent power, it is always valuable, unless it becomes limited to society manners—however good they may be—then it is useless. Nor is actuation of value if one uses it in a routine spirit: doing this and that over and over like a marionette incapable of thought, change or development. For this reason an experimental attitude is an essential attribute of actuation if it is to remain as a constructive therapy.

No habit is a good habit if it remains as an imprisoning channel out of which personality cannot escape. No conduct is good conduct if it constricts progress. Even as one's image-making and autosuggestion should constantly advance in scope and power, so must the behavior patterns established by repetitive actuation continually expand.

Do not allow the thought that you are not being sincere to trouble you, if you act out constructive behavior when you do not feel it natural to do so. You are not your habits but often seem to be. If you are deeply identified with your habits, better habits, created by repetitive action, may not seem to belong to you. A man who has failed continually because of the habit of self-indulgence does not easily identify with the habit of self-discipline. Yet if he repetitively behaves as a self-disciplined person would, and at the same time visualizes controlled conduct, telling himself that discipline is his deliberate choice, the old self-indulgence will gradually give way. Eventually his nerves will take on the new pattern. His reflexes, long conditioned to giving in when effort is required, will gradually become reconditioned. His backbone will stiffen. His glands will function more normally. Even his brain cells will feel a new call to action.

This is the true use of William James's great teaching. Take the pose of a confident, happy person and keep it. When you feel excited do as a calm person would. To teach yourself the work habit keep diligently at a task, even when you are tired. If you do this you will get your "second wind," about which James wrote so reassuringly. Don't yield to the urging of old habits. No matter how you feel, stay with the conduct that you know portrays the good conduct you desire to possess.

I have known of cases where the habit of abusing alcohol was conquered by determined actuation. There are cases where this doing pattern became such a stabilizer of imagery and suggestion as to lead to a definite transformation of a person's life.

Bad habits are subtle things, and those of allowing negative attitudes to control one's thought are the subtlest of all delinquencies. But you can, if you will, persistently behave as if confidence and a conviction of success were yours.

Negativity will only control you if you let it. It ruins your life if you behave like a pessimist. Act as a conqueror and you will conquer.

The actuation process always supposes an inner stimulus such as a desire, a feeling or a motive. A drive in the same way supposes a compelling force. Any impelling implies an inner prompting. You have only then to turn your attention to a personal urge for a better way of life to give power to your actuation. Consider your desires for achievement and for love. They will, if you let them, become invincible motives. By so doing they strengthen your actuation.

During the last world war there were many in Europe who were bombed out of their self-indulgent habits and given new impulses. Circumstances closed off many of the old habits, forcing new drives. Those who experienced this change thereafter possessed creative force. They were impelled by the inner prompting that came as a result of the situational stimulus. With the continued response a permanent actuation developed.

It is good to decide in a definite way what you intend to do.

That, however, is only a start, for "Hell is paved with good intentions." To turn a decision into a means of accomplishment, affirm your actuation to yourself. Affirm it to others. It is easy to give up undeclared intentions, but purposes when stated to others as well as to yourself then involve your pride in a useful way. Others, therefore, involuntarily help you to hold to your decision. Many were they, in the years of my clinical work, who held to their forward steps because their intentions to remain steadfast had been declared to me.

When you have a specific problem to solve, affirm the definite way you intend to deal with it. Let your thinking be as precise as is an architect's blueprint made for a particular house.

When you have no special project, but need to develop and maintain a better morale, use general affirmations of steadfast confidence, for they, too, are concrete designs able to control mental activity. The technique of applied assertion is a true stabilizer of the actuation process.

The splendid work of Doris Marshall in transforming the lives of boys and girls by dramatic training is a magnificent example of how powerful the actuation process can be. She has literally wrought a miracle in Helena, Montana, a miracle that is now spreading to other cities. Control of voice, of gesture, of creative expression are mighty therapies. They release latent powers that gradually become established. The very necessity that a dramatic situation puts upon an actor becomes a means of concentrated effort.

What others have done you can do if you persist. Let me add, however, that there should be no strain, no tension, no painful coercion when you use the actuation process.

Job remarked, ruefully, "My fear has come upon me." Suffering and failure are far too commonly the result of negative anticipation. What one dreads is brought to pass by the

118

unconscious action that accompanies anticipation. It is as if, in our looking ahead, we exemplify in our bodies our thought of what to expect. When our anticipation is haphazard and uncontrolled, worry and anxiety inevitably become the builders of our future experience. It is as if we definitely bring our troubles into being by our mental and physical behavior.

There are those who when told about the power of the actuation process stoutly maintain that they cannot use it successfully. It would be more correct to say that they refuse to change their habits in a constructive way. If that is so, there is no question that they use negative image-making and destructive autosuggestion and allow these injurious processes to block the use of actuation.

No one invented the actuation process. It is not a man-made therapy. Research as to how thought motivates conduct revealed the fact that the organism functions by the activity of reflexes. Conduct patterns develop when a group of reflexes become assembled into habit patterns which then function automatically in many of the operations of the organism.

Actuation most often fails when people *feel* sick but have no disease. The research work of psychosomatic medicine reveals how destructive imagery can cause many of the disfunctions that result in illness. Nor is this injurious process limited to a condition like hypochondria. It is, however, most evident in such cases. It is in a sense a form of negative actuation.

There is only one way to control the destructive effect of fear, worry and anxiety, as they create negative actuation, and that is calmly and persistently to visualize in definite and functional form the constructive behavior of what you wish to bring to pass, how you intend to bring it to pass and why you believe it should be realized.

If you wish to study how mental actuation works, observe it as it appears in the conduct of the Jobs all about you. Listen to what they say, watch what they do, see how their fears come to pass because of the negative behavior in which they indulge. Notice how their lives are literally controlled by an evil pageantry. Then ponder on what the very opposite of this destructive thought would be like. You will then have made a most definite step in the constructive use of actuation.

An actuation pattern is a decision in one's mind of an expression or an activity. It is a way of life or a conduct choice of personality. It is more than a mental image which is only visual. An actuation is tactile as well. A painter places colors on a canvas to represent what he has seen, or conceived, to express an idea. A sculptor adds plastic form, actual three dimensions. His creation is more than a picture. Think so deeply and visualize so fully that your mental images impel an embodiment in actuation. You have experienced dreams that were even more vivid than actual experience. In your dreams the things you touched impressed you much more than the things you saw. The cliffs you climbed on had harsh edges, the streets you trod were sometimes hard and rough. Your dreams were full of sensation because of what you touched. What you saw was intense and striking. But what you felt created a more lasting impression.

Make your thoughts so real that you touch and are touched by their tangible substance. There is no single act that can more fully control your fate than this actualizing of mental imagery.

The actuation process is the eleventh concrete step in the developing of what will ultimately become a single technique for the art of easing out of strain.

12 THE EXPERIMENTAL ATTITUDE

THERE are many remarkable ways in which mental imagery, autosuggestion and actuation can be applied. One does not restrict their use to objective events, such as how the house one longs to possess is achieved, for it is in the subjective realm that these invincible methods possess the most power. They can, in other words, be best used in the application of those constructive therapies that adjust one's behavior to our engineering world.

Many are the readers, as we have said, who respond to some new and sensible idea for better living but do not seem able readily to apply the constructive teaching. This is because they expect that knowing about the new and better way is all that is required to make its use possible. This is not a fact, We need verbally to affirm again and again that we shall persistently use these new and better ways.

Much also depends upon the use of the experimental attitude, to which modern science and mechanical engineering owe most of their advances. Everyone knows of this use of research. They accept it as the point of view of those who have transformed our physical world. They know of the work of various laboratories and testing departments in industry and the universities. They are familiar with the results in their homes, and even in the great achievements the method has made possible in modern medicine. Few are unaware of the fact that the very safety of our nation depends upon the constant inquiries into atomic power that stands at the forefront of our military might.

But how many of such readers ever stop for a moment to apply the experimental attitude to their own way of life? And if, in reading the pages that follow in this chapter, they only read them and do not visualize a personal use of them by creating mental imagery of their functional embodiment, how many will profit by what they read?

It is only as we create for ourselves and in ourselves the sensory equivalents of the great modern means of easier living that we make these dynamic ways part of our own invincible methods of living. We need in our personal lives exactly the spirit that has brought the great objective advancement to pass. We need it in our subjective lives: in the way our minds should work quite as much as in the way our bodies should function.

This same experimental use of attention that is the very heart of science and engineering is also the key to our expanding use of all the therapies. An enthusiasm for them creates mental excitement, which stimulates hope and motivates a belief that accomplishment is possible. This quickening follows the pattern of interest. You may become intrigued by seeing how splendid a garden you can raise or in producing some new species of plants. Perhaps it is manufacturing that enthralls you. You believe you can make better and better products and hope you can win a fortune. You are interested in the development of automation, in machines that do man's work. Or maybe it is one of the arts that holds your attention: new ways of painting or the techniques of the modern stage. Such a field of thought brings you to life. It releases your hidden strengths. Just such a creative urge is needed when using the therapies. When they are impelled by an experimental use of attention their power is invincible. Experimentation of this sort is the way of the greatest of all conquerors. It is persistent research as to how you can actuate your sensory equivalents that leads to accomplishment and the realization of joy.

This is because out of our longings our deep affections are born. No one ever falls in love, or, let us say, he falls only when he stumbles into the illusions of infatuation. Genuine love is the result of developed interests. Nor is this only true in the field of romance. It is quite as true of the love of beauty, of knowledge and of service. Many are they who thought they worshiped some field of effort until they discovered that effort was required. No one truly loves a person he does not know. He does not truly love a subject concerning which he is ignorant. If he weds it, it is from infatuation. A divorce is certain sooner or later. He will give up a subject on which he has not informed himself. This is especially true of one's use of the therapies. Even as hope that leads to inquiry and reveals an increasing interest alone insures the permanence of love, whether it is the love of a boy for a girl or a man for accomplishment, so it is only by continued experimentation that the great therapies become permanent instruments.

There is no greater power in creation than a passion to fulfill some primary aspect of life. It is the electric current that puts a dynamo in the heart of every true procedure. When hope opens the way by dynamic experimentation, revealing the excitement of interests, love appears, for a way of life quite as much as for a person. It does not have to be made. It comes, and with its coming an impelling power brings achievement to pass.

As I have said, most people know it is experimental research that has brought into being the miracles of modern civilization. Let me say again that, knowing this, it is strange how few people use experimentation in their lives.

Consider a man we will call Andrew Berwick. Few of his hopes have been realized. He has gone on in a haphazard manner dreaming of the things he would like in life with little or no gaining of his wishes. Hope for him has always led to frustration. It is as if he expects an invisible power to fulfill his desires without any activity on his part. He asks life to give him what he wants. One wonders what sort of a wife a girl would make who did not have to be wooed and won. What comes too easily is often worthless.

What sort of a career would you expect Andrew to develop with no planning to guide his effort?

We should never forget that in the absence of proven knowledge, all advancement depends upon experiment. He who knows what sort of wife he wants, and already knows the girl and her willingness to marry him, is little likely to become interested in the question of her suitability. If he and his prospective bride are already deeply and actually in love, the issue is closed. But few are so sure of their amorous choice, and they it is who need to consider the importance of compatibility expressed in similar tastes and interests, concordant beliefs and ethical values, equivalent degrees of refinement and intelligence, similar responses of brain, nerves and glands to the stimulus of life.

If there were more experimental research into the actualities of love, the divorce rate would drop to a minimum. So, too, with the question of one's vocation. Success and happiness in a career are quite as dependent on compatibility between the person and his work as in the case of marriage. Nor can we expect true achievement and much joy unless a person's environment is suited to his make-up. Every aspect of life requires analysis as to its affect upon an individual. The lover of a bustling city fares poorly in the wilderness, while he who adores the wooded hills is stifled in urban turmoil.

The experimental attitude then is the only means by which one's place in creation may be successfully discovered. But there is more to this great procedure than that of finding the larger factors in one's life. For experimentation is a basic need if a person is to remain vital and his mental health is to endure. We should learn to inquire into each and every aspect of life as it touches us. What can I do with this situation? How can I deal with that event? Why has this experience come to me? We should learn to meet trouble and good fortune, disturbing problems and joyous happenings, in the experimental spirit that is so characteristic of a well and normal child. Continually he asks himself, "What can I do with this?" "How can I use that?"

Norman Winshaw was born into a family where old habits and routine ways of living had long been entrenched. It was as if what had been must always be. Not until Norman took several science courses in college did his ways of life begin to change. Fortunately, his professors in chemistry, physics and biology were ardent believers in research, and faithful users of the experimental method.

"It was as if blindness was taken from my eyes," Norman explained when telling me his story. "I saw how trouble had haunted our family, and why life was passing us by. And so I began to experiment in the processes of living, as well as in my science classes. I discovered I'd never known the kind of people I needed for friends. I experimented to discover new interests in art, music, literature and the drama. Then a passion for achitecture and gardening hit me, so I took some extension courses in our university. That's where I met Lois. I'd already been questioning myself as to what kind of girls were my sort, and Lois certainly was. I can't tell you how utterly the experimental attitude of modern science changed every aspect of my life. It's at once the most practical and yet the most blessed opener of doors."

"Would you even apply it to the little circumstances and events?" I asked.

"I'd apply it to every moment of a person's life," he stated emphatically. "I once met a Chinese who when you asked him what he thought about anything always answered, 'I go look see.' I've learned to 'go look see' what I can do with all that comes before me and to me in life. Why, I'm even experimenting with the foods I eat and having a whale of a time getting all sorts of healthful and enjoyable meals. And as for my business, it's booming, because I'm always finding new and better ways of doing things."

"You sound as if you are happy," I remarked, a little wryly.

"Happy!" he shouted. "The experimental way of life is the only way to find and to keep happiness."

Years ago a man of great wealth came to me in distress. His marriage was unhappy. The relation to his children was not good. He had lost confidence in himself.

He had, I discovered, been born on a drab little farm in Oklahoma. His father had eked out the barest of livings from an unfriendly piece of dusty soil. Disgusted at the prospect of some day struggling with such an agricultural waste, my client left home before he was of age. He could not accept so stark a life as destiny seemed to have planned for him.

After earning his way through college he went into engineering and then into the skills of the oil industry. He returned one day to visit his aging father. It took only a few glances of his experienced eye to decide that the old farm was priceless oil land. Many millions' worth of crude petroleum came from that hitherto harsh soil.

It did not take me long to use this man's experience as an analogy to reveal to him the state of his own life at that time. He had mastered external circumstances and won a fortune for himself. But he still looked upon that self of his as barren soil.

I was able to reveal to him the wealth he had below the surface appearances of his mind. He was helped to use the experimental attitude as a means of reaching the riches in his depths of being.

He began a new kind of mining, which produced power, happiness and spiritual abundance from within himself. His material riches seemed little in contrast to the gushers of permanent joy and continual satisfaction that became his.

How was this transformation accomplished? First of all, in his personal life he was the victim of wrong habits of thought, acquired in his youth but still controlling his adult life. Because of the fact that in only a short time he must go on a long journey, I could not use any extended analytic research into his early unfortunate conditioning. Desiring to do all I could for him, I was still pressed for time. I was forced to discover a swift, sure means of help.

"You have," I told him, "a back brain, technically called the medulla oblongata. It is sometimes called the old brain, because you share it with the other mammals that have not evolved to human stature. You also have what is called the new brain: the great cerebral hemispheres, and that amazing mass of protoplasm, your frontal lobes. This new brain the animals do not possess. The new brain is the instrument of experimental thought, of self-command and of freedom from early, unfortunate experiences.

"The old brain is the receiver of conditioning. It is the

maker of habit. It can and has controlled you and injured your deeper desires by the rulership of negative behavior patterns that it has imposed upon you. This domination need not continue, unless you want it to. Stop. Stop now and begin to live experimentally in your personal life, even as you did in the oil industry. Revulsion is half of cure, a change of attention the rest of it. Refuse to be dominated by the habits of your old brain. You have been acting as if you, too, were as barren as the surface soil of your father's ranch. You have not turned your attention experimentally to discover and use the riches in your great, cerebral hemispheres, or the self-directive power of your frontal lobes.

"All maladjustment can be simplified as a fixation, deflection and deficiency of attention. Your attention has been fixed on the old, melancholy habits that have formed in your old brain. Your attention has been deflected from experimental thinking because of the experiences that are now past and gone. Let the dead past go. Turn your attention onto research in order to seek the wealth in your new brain. Identify yourself as a human being who *has* this new brain. You will then cease to be controlled by the old brain that you share with the animal kingdom."

"How shall I do this?" he asked.

"By applying to your personal life the experimental methods of science and engineering and a very simple self-reminding process. Years ago, when I was a small boy, my father pointed out to me the sort of sign that used to be placed at every railroad crossing: Stop—Look—and Listen. 'That is very important advice,' my father told me, 'placed there to save your life and to avoid injury. It is important that you should learn to use it in all the serious or dangerous activities of your life. Stop, look and listen for the new ideas and better ways your brain will suggest to you.'"

128

My client smiled with sudden understanding. "That's what I did, didn't I, when I realized the wealth hidden under the poor soil of my father's farm? I turned my attention away from the morbid rebellion that he had and the habit of blaming God for our ill luck. I put my attention experimentally on seeking the hidden wealth, and found it."

"Exactly," I cried in relieved response. "And remember this, that in your new brain is a wealth far beyond that which lay below your father's ranch. In your new brain is creative power and the capacity for constructive research, made possible by memory, reason, imagination, the power of judgment and the capacity for decision. It also possesses the instinct of curiosity. That is the seeker of wisdom. From its use has come all the miracles of modern science."

"I know that, of course," he answered solemnly. "What a fool I've been. But, you see, this point is so simple that it has escaped me. I've won my wealth by the experimental use of my new brain and let my old brain dominate my personal life, ruin my marriage and—well—and all the rest of it. But, by thunder, I'm not going to let my old habits enslave me any longer. I'll stop, stop short, when the old brain tries to trick me. I won't let it deflect my thought and make me deficient in my attention to the finer guidances of my mind."

There is no greater, simpler or surer way to transform your life than to stop, look and listen, seeking the experimental processes of your mind. At every crossroads of thought, at every blind turn in your life experience, experiment. Stop your thoughtless involvement in the rush of events; look calmly and carefully at the situation; then listen, listen quietly, to the deeper guidances that rise up in your consciousness to help you. If you are attentive to the experimental process, and shut out for a little time the noise of life, you will receive great help. For you will then use research to create newer and better sensory equivalents of your true desires.

Let us remind ourselves that all great truths are simple; all the knowledge of how to apply wisdom simpler still. Then let us not ignore these *hows*, that built this nation and gave it strength. Let us use them to set us free of the stress that destroys our health and happiness.

The use of this thoughtful method to discover and to apply sensory equivalents is the twelfth step in the conquest of strain.

13 CREATIVE ENERGY

$\mathcal{I}$N YOUR youth you possessed the three greatest of gifts: your ruling hopes, your ruling interests and your ruling loves. These are the gems beyond price that the world sells so cheaply in barter for tinsel contentments. They were made vital by your enthusiasm and they controlled your energies.

At adolescence there were in your heart not one but several of these impellings. They were, in the large, longings for the fulfillment of your true wants. This was so even if you were not mature enough to know what an ideal value was. Your desires were a spontaneous urge. You wished to be able to do something in life that, as it were, just *did itself*. You felt that maybe you had abilities that would work for you without undue effort. You did not wish to push and strain as the adults around you said you must.

By sixteen you may have lost the belief that life could be

lived without drudgery. If so, you were rebelling along with the so-called "wild teenagers," or else buckling down to the delusion that life was only a drab routine. In any case, some of your hopes for adventure, for achievement, for love, for the excitement of success may have disappeared.

Along with this loss of the springs of eternal youth your ruling interests could also have been dimmed. What was it that intrigued you? That you had ruling interests is certain, unless you were a very strange youth.

I recall a discouraged bond salesman who as a boy of eleven wanted to sell tin pans in the street. His father, an American bank official in Paris, had brought the boy up in Montmartre, where bright, shiny pans were marketed by means of a peddler's musical cry. Helped to discover and return to his basic interest, that bond salesman became an actor in musical comedy, an adult activity that had the same sparkle as that of a singing tinsmith marching through a vivid crowd with its gaiety and nonchalance. How could a man who loved a Paris throng be happy peddling the wares of Wall Street?

One's ruling interests, like one's ruling hopes, are true motivating centers urging to a healthy and happy life, even when they appear in infantile form. What thrilled you as a child? What thrills you now? What things, events, activities and thoughts quicken the feelings of your heart and speed the surge of your blood? Whatever they are, they belong to you, and loyalty to them is an essential factor in true adjustment.

Nor are your ruling loves less essential. They can, in fact, be used to correct your faults and failings. Once you discover some primary passion of your being, you will not carry on conduct that threatens or injures it. I have known men to give up an excessive use of alcohol, in fact, any and every sort of delinquency, when the realization came to them that a ruling love was thereby injured.

132

It does not suffice, however, to be told that the possession of hopes, interests and ruling loves is important to us. We must know how to regain them, how to keep them and how to use them, as motive powers of our lives.

Just what is hope, and how is it brought into being? Hope results from an ability we have as human beings to see beyond the situations and difficulties with which we are confronted. The hopeless person stares so hard at his troubles he sees nothing else. His thought is fixed, in a belief that unconquerable obstacles are in his way. His attention is swallowed, as it were, by negative anticipation. He is thus deficient in purpose, for purpose is empowered by hope, interest and love. In contrast, the hopeful man refuses to yield to the pressure of circumstances. His thought is experimental. He seeks information as to how the situation may be changed.

This experimental use of attention, as we have already said, is the most important and most valuable of all man's possessions. From it has come all that has eased our lives. Out of it sprang the very soul of civilization. From the use of it in your life success and happiness are born.

It is not difficult to trace the power of the experimental use of attention back to prehistoric days. The men who made the first boats were tired of paddling heavy rafts. They experimented by hollowing out a log. The resulting contraption was easier to move. Someone held up the branch of a tree. The wind blew against it and the idea of a sail was born.

Hope for easier ways of travel then surged in men's minds. Hope urged on the experiments. Hope quickened the research from century to century until at last an airplane came into being.

Hope is developed by the experimental use of attention and maintained by persistent research. This, let me repeat for the sake of emphasis, is the spirit that motivates the great laboratories of science, engineeriing and industry. It is the impelling power behind the advancement of medicine. It is the source of all progress.

When you and I realize this fact and also apply it, our personal lives become transformed whatever our problems may be. We then know that there is just one thing to do, namely, to carry on hopeful research, persistently to experiment until a solution, in the form of a practical action, comes to pass. Experiments lead to a sudden expansion of consciousness, a deeper perception, a new angle. This is the way to mental health and a return to the spirit of youth.

A careful study of the lives of fortunate people reveals the fact that they let nothing dim their hopes, interests and loves, nor permitted anything to stand in the way of the fulfillment of these primary longings. They refused the demands and abnegations the bigots of virtue have striven to force upon us all.

Life *can* become an adventure full of the excitement of conquest. Time to play and the realization of pleasure can be ours. From knowing how to work without strain we win for ourselves ample times of rest. The cycle of adventure out into the world is then a fulfillment of all that means satisfaction.

Those who tell us life must be a dirge speak either from ignorance or else to hold us in subservience. The tragedy, however, is that many believe their desires for an easier way of life are wrong. Were you not taught that you must work hard, and, while your companions slept, toil upward in the night? If you weren't, those about you were.

You have only to read the moral aphorisms of the last century to prove it. To many of our forefathers a happy way of life seemed evil. Maybe in your youth you dimly felt their admonitions were antiquated. But no one taught you that we each and all have a right to follow our hopes, to protect our interests and to fulfill our loves. Our training was quite to the contrary.

There is, for this reason, no greater guide to release from strain than the way it was achieved by those who accomplished great things in the laboratory of life, despite the bad counsel they received. Henry Ward Beecher declared: "Greatness lies not in being strong, but in the right using of strength." To this Churchill added: "Genius is independent of situation," a modern application of the great words of Casanova: "Life leads its lover, betrays its rebel."

Certain of the moralists have taken issue with the way the geniuses won their way to greatness. They point out that the lives of our heroes were far from heroic in their *personal* relations. Others emphasize the evidences of selfishness as if it were the sin of sins. *All of them miss the point.*

We are not here concerned with the ethics of their conduct. It must, of course, be considered in due time, but not until we understand what we are measuring. Hasty moralizing belongs to men of small minds. Neither life nor the force which created it can be squeezed into a precept and not become vapid.

There are values that are large and others that are small. The little ones belong to little people, content with diminutive living. The larger values are for you, *if* you are discontented in the lock step of a routine existence.

There is a point here in our study of easing out of strain that is of major importance, and that is as to the nature of selfishness. Successful desire is organized, is it not, on the only basis that ever permits success, which is a primeorderliness of effort for the fulfillment of one's hopes, interests and loves?

There is nothing wrong with the way selfishness is set up. It is built, shall we say, like a plow, with the plowshare in the lead: that is, *one* most important desire is put first. This is sustained by *two* or more significant, but slightly less important, wants and fortified by a number of impelling but not as essential cravings. So, back and back the structure goes, as sturdy as a pyramid, its power greater than all other formative designs.

If you put the tips of your two hands together, both pointed downward, you construct an inverse form, a valley or cone, into which anything that is dropped will lodge. This is the goody-goody catch-all pattern by which patient failures are burdened down with the duties of others. The load they carry is equal to the pack on Pilgrim's back. Invert the position of your hands so that the tips point upward. You have established a structure with slanting sides. No object, if dropped on your hands when so arranged, can lodge. It falls off. Likewise duties and responsibilities that are not rightfully yours will not be assumed if your desires are organized in this efficient manner.

Not only is the way of life of the selfish person formed like a pyramid, it is the structural secret of all good fortune. It is also, sentimentalists to the contrary, the means by which all great service has ever been accomplished. A man dedicated to social advance must be as obedient to this principle, as faithful to his hopes, interests and loves, and as enthusiastic in the release of his energy as the most greedy of misers and the most avaricious of shrews.

Selfishness then is formed in the right way but for the wrong aim. It is evil when its purposes are evil. It is not evil in its method of gaining results. If a man's motives are those of co-operation and mutual aid, he has aims utterly opposite from those of selfishness. If, however, he is to succeed, and good fortune is to attend his efforts to serve his fellow man, he must obey the law of primeorderliness and be as invincibly steadfast in his spirit as Croesus himself.

Primeorderliness is a way of life that is necessary to all worthwhile living. The term designates a practice of choosing the most essential thought or action in any situation that requires decision and of putting it first in order in one's procedure. No values in life are fully realized without a comprehension and use of this element of choice, of putting that thing first which properly belongs first, and arranging the other essential steps in sensible order: second, third, fourth and so on down the line.

Much has been said in recent decades about personal adjustment, most of it on the basis of compromise. It is obvious that the great accomplishers have held to an entirely different standard: adjustment of circumstances to them, rather than adjustment of themselves to circumstances. They have instinctively understood an emphasizing of the major values or what seemed so to them.

Would you rather have had Wagner absorbed in being an exemplary man or in being a great composer? Would it have been better for him to "wear prayer books in his pockets and swear but now and then," and thus have used up the concentration he needed to compose dynamic music? Being made in the way he was, had he absorbed his creativity in an obedience to the moral precepts of his day and age he would have written only sentimental and silly songs. Being a Siegfried with battles to win, he wrote the music of inner conquest and power. Make your choice between a weak and simpering goodness or a life of heroic achievement. Biography reveals that they do not go together. At least they never have.

Let us face the facts. Some people win power, position, love, joy, money, a fine home, pleasure, great accomplishment, adventure, excitement, service. Few gain all, some satisfy one or more, others many, of their insatiable wants. Let me repeat that whether or not they do it by a means that is right or wrong is not what we are as yet considering. The point is that they used a way that won. The skill by which an eagle catches a rabbit is still an eagle's prowess, no matter who may sit in judgment on the ethics of his act. And is it not true that he lives or dies dependent upon the efficiency of his swoop to earth? The point is that some people get a lot out of life and put a joyous amount into it. Even if we later on consider the ethics of their art, we need first to know what the art is.

Three points are then before us.

1. Is it only from selfishness that some people succeed and others fail, even when they had energy and enthusiasm, or is it also a matter of greater brains and ability? History and biography prove that it is neither of these.

2. *How* they achieved is revealed to be the great but simple art of primeorderliness, acting through sensory equivalents. It was *the means they followed* in the use of their gifts that brought their realizations to pass.

3. What they did to *fulfill* their desires becomes the aim of our research if we would also live transcendently.

Can fate be in some measure controlled? Is it true that there are acts which can direct one's way to the top and circumvent the dirge of destiny? As we progress in our research it will show that there are; that the great and near great used these means, instinctively, intuitively or unconsciously—choose which word you will. Their conclusions as to how victory can be accomplished may have differed, but none of them doubted that it could be done.

Of one fact we can be sure: that those who won positions of power, who gained recognition, who performed great services for mankind, who sought and found love, who, in whatever their sphere, became fortunate, maintained through thick and thin an affirmative attitude concerning the desires they sought to fulfill. They may have lost hope, interest and love concerning *one* aspect of life but never toward *all*. In the area wherein their achievement took place, hope, interest and love were invincible. "He that loses hope," wrote Congreve, "may part with anything."

Enough nonsense has been written in behalf of affirmation, however, to cover the earth. It has been portrayed as an attitude that "all's right with the world." All isn't. Much is wrong. No matter what a muddled mess it is, however, there is order behind it, and the very existence of success in any life proves that there is some place where sane effort will overcome the chaos.

Plenty of the great men of business had little optimism as to the saintliness of their fellow man but an unyielding affirmative as to their power to do business. There have been scientific men who had little faith in humanity but utter belief in cosmic law. Nothing limited the affirmative attitude they held as to what science is and what it can do. Many an artist has half starved in his garret, sure that he could paint. When his attitude was unyielding he won to the fullest that his endowment made possible. If he lost an affirmative confidence he failed, even with a major gift.

It is then an invincible affirmative in some one area of one's life for the fulfillment of some hope, interest or love that is essential. The rest of one's experience can remain a muddle. But if that muddle is forced aside by an enthusiasm for some one aim, and a central hope, interest or love is loyally maintained for that aim, conquest results. Nor is this all. Achievement at this one spot often releases such energy and faith that all the rest of life, even the muddled part of it, is neutralized and becomes less burdensome.

This is by no means a thoughtless process. To discover and use a hope, an interest or a love, or all of them together, requires constructive contemplation. This is a kind of conversation with oneself, a talking things over with the only person who listens patiently. Only you can think your way through. You do it only by quiet and deep meditation. Thereby you achieve needed self-direction.

He who contemplates his desires long and thoroughly comes to understand them. Remaining loyal to them he keeps faith in them no matter how ridiculous they at first appear. He learns by this autosuggestional meditation how to give them constructive fulfillment. That is what the great accomplishers have done, intuitively. By this means what they hoped to achieve became clarified so that a definite and practical way to accomplish it came to pass. You and I, using the evidence they have left to us of this sturdiness of purpose, can thereby consciously and intentionally fulfill our aims.

In this reference, there is a word of great importance here that has long been neglected in our common speech. That word is acturience. It combines in its meaning an impelling for active fulfillment of one's hopes, interests and dominant loves. Socrates had an acturience for truth, Shakespeare for drama, Martin Luther for political-religious liberty, Abraham Lincoln for the rights of human brotherhood.

The great men of science possessed acturience for cosmic knowledge. The major artists were impelled by acturience to create beauty. Andrew Carnegie was driven by acturience to industrial organization and conquest.

Acturience is not only a long-neglected word but a way of life too seldom followed. Acturience means that one has maintained into adult life the adventure drive so characteristic of a child. It is a desire to do, to keep on doing, trying to satisfy curiosity, to remain forever unsatisfied with what is or has been. The energy that fulfills one's ruling hopes, interests and loves comes from acturience at work. Great is the power and the worth of discontent, when one's life is shaped on less than one's rights for the gaining of natural desires.

Whatever divinities you reverence, the great accomplishers worshiped that sturdy god, Keepatit. But do not for a moment believe that that means routine toil. The great god Keepatit is more like a sitting Buddha than an industrious puritan. He is not afraid of the temptations of rest and play. There is delight in doing what one's hopes designate, one's interests impel and lure one to do. Passionate desire helps one to concentrate on what is important to one's personal being, and deliciously to ignore the millions of duties that others would pour upon one's head.

This requirement most obviously means that a method, which we call dynamic organization, must close the door on failure and direct one's effort to definite ends.

The biographies of the great achievers and especially the statements in their letters and diaries startlingly reveal their experience with spontaneous accomplishment. It was as if a surge of thought, feeling and activity rose within them, flowing through long-established habit paths into automatic constructiveness.

Many are they who, like Goethe, spoke of a godlike power that carried them to great accomplishment. As with Socrates, Goethe had his "demon," capable of far greater achievement than he, without such a dynamic energy, could ever have produced. Voltaire, Stevenson and many of the artists and composers possessed this divine impelling. It empowered most of the inventors, and men of science have given lasting testimony to a magnificent force, latent in all, active in them, that in an effortless way brought their purposes to pass.

14 REPETITIVE STRATEGY

*A*N EQUIVALENT is not, of course, limited to the creating of changes in an individual's mental or physical state; it is equally useful in the achievement of goals. It empowers one to realize what he wants so fully that the behavior of how to acquire it becomes clarified.

It was as if a fresh sea breeze blew away all of Horace Ardmor's old doubts when he discovered this modern method. "I was," he told me, "a bank clerk for years and how I hated it. To console myself I used to go to the movies to see westerns and read all the books I could get of ranch life. But it never occurred to me to do anything to get out of the bank and the city. But when I learned about sensory equivalents I began to realize powerfully the sort of life I wanted and the kind of ranch I had secretly longed to own. That made me do something about it. I bought books and maps; I took a course in animal husbandry and read up on crop management.

That did it. My sensory cquivalents then began to take form, and you know the rest. The drive in me then became so strong I inevitably found my ranch, and I was also ready to make it succeed!"

To some degree this need for concrete action has long been understood. François Delsarte taught it by saying: "The object of art is to crystallize emotion into thought and then to fix it in form. All living is an art if experience is well lived. It comes to pass when purpose is appropriately embodied, a plan constructively fulfilled." "There is great affinity between design and art," wrote Addison. "Without design art fails even for those especially well endowed." This is a truth that Gambetta applied even in the controlling and organizing of men. "Great ability without discretion comes almost invariably to a tragic end," he stated. He did not realize, however, and his life story proves it, that one could over-organize the expressions of ability by too much conscious effort and not enough affirmativeness in one's attitude. "Dangers are light if they seem light," wrote Bacon, "and more dangers have deceived men than have faced them."

It is true, as Theodore Parker put it, that, "Genius is the father of a heavenly line, but the mortal mother, that is industry." This idea was better expressed by Eschenback when she wrote: "Genius points the way, talent pursues it." This is well said if, and only if, talent continues to see where genius points. It is unfortunate that more often than not it doesn't.

"We encourage one another in mediocrity," Charles Lamb admonished. Talent tends to do this from fear of the scope of genius. Bovee cried out against this sacrifice of greatness, saying: "We trifle when we set limits to our desires since nature has set none." George Macdonald went still further when he wrote: "There is no inborn longing that shall not be fulfilled."

What a magnificent optimism! Must it be only that? Is it true? Yes, and no. Yes, if one knows how to fulfill his longings by the use of sensory equivalents; no, if there is no formative process. Our desires will not become realized unless a campaign is established, as Wellington had done before the Battle of Waterloo. One must develop and use his own repetitive techniques. The process consists in seeking to contact again your basic purposes, then by an active use of experimental imagery do all you can to set those dynamic forces free as motive centers of your life.

Such powers are never lost. They are only buried under dull, gray, adult attitudes of compromise. You can, when you wish to do so, rediscover them. You can, if you will, release and strengthen them. Even if for a while you use your longings only in an avocation, you will have made a start. And if, like a general who plans his moves, you mull out an organized active effort that uses your primary urgings, you will—in a time shorter than you can believe—become a dynamically going concern. Soon everyone will think of you as a person of achievement and exceptional worth.

There are seven major wants of the human spirit. While each of us wants them all, and many minor ones, we tend to accent a special or particular quality of wanting in our psychic yearning. First, some people's wants are of a material nature; they especially desire good clothing, shelter, money, position. Some have wants of action: sports, adventure, motion, conquest. Still others primarily crave social interchange: emotional contacts, sensation, being with people and sustained by them. Then there are those who long for intellectual understanding, knowledge, science. A few yearn for altruistic realization, ethical fulfillment, service, to give and to receive nurture. Fewer still are those who seek creativity, idealism, aesthetic expression, beauty, art, music, literature, design, to understand cosmic order. Lastly, there are those whose upreachings are for the spiritual values, who desire psychological understanding, philosophical insight, knowledge of the meaning of life, religious ecstasy.

More nonsense has been written, I believe, on the subject of our wants than on any other aspect of life. The old Puritans were emphatic about self-denial and seemed to believe that one should never expect to fulfill his desires. They taught that this is a world of discipline and disappointment. Even intelligent men of science have sometimes sounded as if too much of what they called "determinism" stood in the way of our longings to have them ever come true.

Mankind, on the other hand, and youth especially, has gone right on hoping and dreaming of unbounded wealth, perfect love and magnificent ideals. And isn't it a fact that most authors, even those who don't write fairy tales, give us a happy ending?

What is the truth of this riddle? Can we intelligently hope to have our longings come to pass? Most of us would give a fortune for the answer.

A good many years ago I dreamed that some day I would like to have a beautiful home in an ideal climate, with sea beaches, great trees and snow-capped mountains to look at. There was to be a cove for a fast cruiser, a swimming pool and a greenhouse. Most of all, the house was to have great fireplaces, with plenty of snapping logs to burn. I preferred, I decided, arched windows of leaded glass, and great doors with hand-wrought hinges. The sun porch was to look out across blue water, dotted with verdant islands to the dazzling snow of the surrounding mountains. Just for good measure, silver salmon would splash in the calm waters and brown deer wander in the woods.

You will admit that, not being in any sense a man of wealth,

I was a good hand at wanting things. Many a fairy tale isn't half as full of such utter desire. My friends, of course, looked upon my longing as completely impossible and crazily idealistic. "There just isn't any such perfect place in the United States," they said. "Be sensible. You might find a bit of seashore, but not along with snow-capped mountains; or if you get near to a mountain, you would have to live in a dark valley. Then too a professional man such as you are could never build or buy a house like that." As I described it in detail, they told me it was more like a palace than a poor man's cottage.

So my friends laughed and told me to come down to earth. They'd "never dream" of trying to find a home like that. I'm sure they wouldn't. Anyway, they don't own a home like that —and I do. That's the funny part of it, but it's my fun. Yes, I'm the one who owns a mile and a quarter of lovely waterfront with beautiful sea beaches, from which I look out past verdant islands to the snow-capped mountains of the Northwest. And my house has arched, leaded glass windows, with great fireplaces, and there are six hundred and forty-four acres of woods and fields, all mine to work and play in.

I wonder which of us was the more practical: my friends who laughed and thought me a little daft, or I, who got just what I wanted. But how? What did I do to make my dream come true? If I told you I just used visual imagery you would have a right to be disgusted. Just the same, that was the first part of what I did. But I also used suggestion and the actuation process. Having made a very clear picture in my mind of what I very much wanted, I then trained myself to be able to achieve it. I acted as if such a place belonged to me, that it would be my right. I dramatized my desire to myself and tactfully to others, and thereby gained their help.

I talked and talked as interestingly as I could about the place I wanted. Gradually one person after another told me about seacoasts and mountains, good climates and salmon fishing. In my spare time I pored over encyclopedias, maps and geographies. When I could, I spent my vacations looking for the spot that would fulfill my dreams.

The major step in such a repetitive strategy is to make so strong a sensory equivalent of what you want that you and everyone you know helps you to find it. The second step is to keep on and on, actuating your desire, even against ridicule and disappointment. That is what I had to do. Then one day I found the very spot, the sea beach, the snow-capped mountain views, and even the house with leaded glass windows, set so as to look out on laughing water full of jumping salmon.

When I found it, I learned the building was brand-new and had cost much money. How was I, a professional man who earns about what he spends each year, ever to have a place like that? I didn't despair. I'd made friends with a real estate man, who lived in the region. I told him about my dream, and of the property I had seen. Then I went back to my city life miles away. Six months passed. One day the aftermath of the crash of 1929 reached such a crisis that the owner of that property wanted to sell at almost any price. He needed the money to hold his equity in his business. Like an explosion I received a telegram. If I could send a rather small sum of money before nightfall, I could have the property. I could. I did. I bought it free and clear. Was it just luck? I don't think so. In fact, I know it wasn't.

Months afterward, when I found there was not a flaw in my purchase and all my longings were realized, the real estate man remarked, "You know, Seabury, even with the banks closed in this state, I think I could have found the money to buy that place myself. But you'd given me such a picture of the home you longed to have, I just had to let it go to you."

There is an important principle here that very few people

147

seem to understand. It consists in letting yourself passionately realize your own desires and the exuberance you have about them. "Nothing is so contagious as enthusiasm," wrote Bulwer-Lytton. "It moves stones, it charms brutes. Enthusiasm is the genius of sincerity and truth accomplishes no victories without it." Longfellow taught the same lesson in fewer words: "Enthusiasm begets enthusiasm." Fuller knew that we must, however, use our warmth of feeling through action. "Lose not thine own for want of asking for it. 'Twill get thee little thanks."

In my case I received thanks for my asking. The man from whom I bought my house saved his fortune because I acted so quickly. In gratitude he returned to me some of the equipment and things he had taken out to sell. I deserved to have them, he wrote. So everyone was happy.

In order to clear one's mind of the compromising of one's wants which the years may have created, a definite method is necessary. We must clarify Repetitive Strategy and construct it into a working process. This is done by the technique of the Adaptation Point.

Let us picture three little tables in a row. On the first table, at the extreme left, we will put the hard facts of life, of *any person's life*: the toil he is engaged in, his personal limitations of brains, beauty or brawn, the amount of his money or his lack of it, the limitations of his environment, the opportunities he has or hasn't, all that pertains to his situation.

Now, on the table at the other end, the extreme right, we will put the elements of a fairy tale: all the wants and desires one ever had, the plans and purposes from childhood and youth that existed before the adult days we miscall maturity. There is to be no limit to the longings placed upon this right-hand table. One can dream as if he had unlimited intelligence, any or every ability in its fullest form, abundant charm and opportunities without stint. There is to be no question as to one's riches, in money or other possessions, for this is a fairy tale that knows no limits.

Next we will turn our attention to the central table, which is to become the adjustment point. One is to look back and forth between the left- and the right-hand tables: that is, the one that holds the hard facts of life and the one that holds the dreamlike fairy tale. One then considers how far one can *at that time* lift the hards facts of life toward a fulfillment of the fairy tale. There should be no compromise of essential values in making the decision.

If in the fairy tale love, truth, beauty, goodness and courtesy were essential values, they are not surrendered or submerged by the forces and strictures caused by the hard facts of life on the left-hand table. All compromise is refused. One must adapt, and one may have to wait, but he still will make no important relation without love—in marriage, for example—until the time comes when the hard facts can be more successfully adjusted to the values of the fairy tale. It is better to go without than to surrender any of the cosmic realities.

Practice in the use of the adaptation point between the extremes of the hard facts and the insatiable longings gives one a habit of effort and a constant increase in power and wisdom. Strain, either from compromise or from unsatisfied mechanical idealism, is greatly reduced. One comes down to earth, but without any loss of his impelling desires. As one learns how to adjust, more and more of the fairy tale becomes realized and gradually forms a greater measure of a person's life.

As I sit here writing I am in the beautiful house that countless people told me I could never own. Many other hopes have come true, not all at once but as rapidly as life and my use of techniques permitted their realization. I have gradually raised the quality and quantity of what was on my central table, my adaptation point, until more and more of my longings and desires have been realized. Nor have I stopped "dreaming" by any means. There are still great urgings I have to fulfill. My adaptation point will go higher and higher.

I could write a dozen books on the power and practicality of the adaptation point for the realization of one's deeper purposes. I could make long lists of how it has produced what people call "miracles." You have only to try it and practice its use until you are skilled in handling it, to know that knowledge in connection with Repetitive Strategy is greater than the wealth of Midas.

However individual our desires may be, two primary drives motivate every human life, the urge for self-expansion and for the realization of love. Whatever of your wants and wishes you handle haphazardly, do not neglect the thoughtful concern needed to assure your place in life, and your achievement of compatible companionship. Every little child is impelled by an adventure spirit, an impulse to experience life to the full. It once was yours. It still is, even if now hidden. Begin today to design your life so that more of your longings are fulfilled.

A wise businessman plans a sales campaign and prospers only because he does so. Stop to survey your life. In order to avoid idle fantasy and purposeless dreams, use a pencil and paper to write concrete lists. What do you want? Why do you want it? How do you plan to gain it? Who do you know who can help you? Where are those who might be willing to assist? When should you begin your campaign?

Successful lives are designed on the same principles as a reciprocating engine: a give and then a take, a give and then a take, and so on and on in a majestic momentum. In an engine the steam or exploding gas gives a shove to the piston and then takes in more of the powerful vapor. You and I must also find sources from which we can replenish our energy after each expenditure of effort.

Some people, however, are not careful to organize their lives so that they can take what they need for each act of giving. If you don't keep the give and take in balance, you will soon become exhausted and be unable to give.

If you do not at this time have your taking as well as your giving well established, stop giving for a while and take time to think. Wait—and think and think until you have reorganized your experience. Reciprocation is a basic law of successful living. This is not selfishness, it is the way of intelligence.

Planning fulfills intents and purposes. It is an adjustment of actions to accomplish aims. All performance requires an unfolding design if it is to be adequately executed.

As a final step in the development of Repetitive Strategy, let me suggest that there is no single act that can more affect your way of life than to attempt to write the story of your next ten years. Anyone can write the autobiography of the decade he has just passed through. You cannot, of course, with any certainty, write such an autobiography of the years ahead, but to attempt to do so clarifies your purposes quite as definitely as a house is visualized by an architect. If you attempt to think out the story of the days to be, you will transform your relation to them. You will avoid doing many things you would otherwise have done, and you will deliberately do many things you might otherwise have neglected. You can, if you will, be the director of your destiny.

This method of controlling your fate by repetitive strategy is the fourteenth step in the art of living without tension.

15   THE ART OF MOMENTARY LIVING

*I*N ORDER fully to clear our minds that we may successfully use the modern means for the conquest of events, we must give definite attention to the thinking processes which scientific men have applied to the solving of problems. Their use of them, let us admit, has often been unconscious, but the methods are not less important for all that.

Seldom can you convince the dubious doubters that it is practical to have faith in good fortune or confidence in the coming of a better destiny. Tell them that you believe that we are, in the large, treated by life according to our own attitude toward it in thought, feeling and action and these seers of doom fairly froth at the mouth, as if your hope were a sappy sentimentality. But, we might ask, must we bring up every danger, and see every possibility of sickness, sorrow and disaster which this doctrine of their kind of "practicality" implies?

The truth of the matter is that there is only one time and place wherein you can apply what you learned from the mistakes in the past that will insure a better future, and that is in the present. This fact millions have had dinned into them in platitudes and moralistic verse. "Act, act in the living present." But the admonition has emphasized doing, and not careful planning. We in America need no more admonitions to keep us nervously moving. An itch to action has long been our substitute for thoughtfulness.

The philosophy of momentary living is not an escape from intelligent foresight, nor yet an ignoring of the wisdom that past experience may have contained. It is a belief that today is the time in which we can correct the unfortunate momentums the past may have set in motion. If we control the events of today by good sensory equivalents and wise decisions, we determine, in the large, what tomorrow is to become.

There is an old truism which says: "Don't worry about results; correct the causes." In our modern psychological vernacular we say: "If you give your attention to creating the best sequences that you now can, you will bring the best consequences to pass that you can later on possess." "Don't be anxious about consequences, give your attention to designing good sequences."

This is such magnificent advice that nearly everyone who reads it nods his head and is sure he agrees. He does so in theory. Yet millions of those who think they understand this teaching rarely apply it in their lives. Yet it was by this means that our mechanical age came into being and each invention was conceived.

A sequence is a design, a plan or arrangement of thought, feeling and action. It is a purposive pattern, a combination of sensory equivalents deliberately chosen, to establish a certain way of life. To the creating of it we should give such concentrated attention that we need not worry as to what the outcome will be.

Even a simple use of logic should reveal to anyone that all consequences are the effect of the sequences of thought, feeling and action that brought them to pass. No consequences can be better or worse than the arrangements of sensory equivalents that are used in the control of external events.

To many people this statement does not seem to be true because there are forces at work in the life around us which are beyond our control. These disasters are spoken of as "acts of God." Earthquakes, hurricanes, droughts, floods, lightning. The obscurities of darkness, time and space are factors also that we do not create. They are, however, elements with which we must deal, nor can we ignore the limitations of man, the depressions and wars of nations, the social ignorances and stupidities.

Let us admit then that no one can produce an inevitable philosophy or a psychic economy that does not consider the facts and the forces of life that exist beyond ourselves. At the same time, the world would never even have approached the civilization it now possesses, had not a little knowledge been able to overcome and eradicate a great deal of ignorance. By thoughtful experiment man has been able to modify and to some degree eliminate the difficulties of life that confronted him in prehistoric times. Just to the degree that he turned his attention to the making of sensory equivalents for the erection of activities capable of conquering the difficulties, those possibilities became probabilities and then evolved into constructive and certified outcomes.

What has been true of the life of man in his conquest of the earth is true of your life and mine. It is the secret of success in our personal efforts. To the degree that our intelligence is locked in a dread of the results of what we do in a world still full of primitive men and primordial forces, to that degree we shall reap the dirge of misfortune.

Let us repeat for the sake of emphasis. To the extent that we stalwartly create good equivalents of the best sequences of thought, feeling and action that we can conceive in any given moment, and embody our considered purposes in a deliberate effort; to that degree, no matter what the situation is, or what forces of nature—human or otherwise—are involved, we shall achieve the best consequences that can, under the circumstances, be brought to pass.

When such a philosophy, which is also a practical psycho-economy, is established and repetitively used, it reduces difficulties to the least possible number and greatly modifies strain. Man loves a struggle and is bored by a life of supine placidity. He revels in conquest, when he is free to fight intelligently and knows where to put his attention.

Concern for the establishment of good and practical sequences of thought, feeling and action is the only concern that is not destructive. It shakes up a situation as efficiently as a cat worries a rat.

Anxiety as to whether or not one is breaking out of self-indulgence long enough to establish operational equivalents is the real issue. The organizing of an intelligent campaign of conquest takes no toll from nerves or glands. Foresight that stops to see what to do, how to do it and why it should be done, not only organizes constructive equivalents but the successful activities of any situation as well.

For years Henry Mallard was in delicate health. The doctors told him that the condition of his heart was "serious," because his blood pressure was so high. He was also toxic and given to constipation. His tension was so great that people said, "It makes me nervous just to be with him." He did not do anything wrong exactly or say anything in particular to create this atmosphere, but people felt it. Even his wife and children found reason to be where he wasn't most of the time.

Then came the inevitable "nervous breakdown" and a six months' visit to a sanitarium. It was the most fortunate experience that ever came to Henry and it saved his life.

The psychiatrist assigned to talk with him was a woman, which fact did not disturb him at first. After all, he was an only son whose father had died while he was in his teens. An anxious mother and three older sisters had long ago conditioned Henry to listen patiently when one or more of the feminine sex was talking, and in his family that was constantly. He therefore accepted a woman psychiatrist quite graciously.

But when she started to discuss his business worries with him Henry struck, that is he attempted insurrection for part of an interview. What did she know about business, he demanded, as a challenging opening. Well, she told him, after graduating from college she'd been a file clerk at first, then a stenographer. This was followed by a year of bookkeeping while she started her premed training. She then earned her way through medical school doing special assignments for a large advertising company, cashing in most efficiently on the fact she had specialized in psychology during her college years. "After I got my medical degree I felt the need of a Ph.D., and that was made possible by a year's assignment doing some work for the Department of Commerce."

"That's quite a list," Henry admitted. "Sounds efficient."

"Don't you see," she countered, "*you've* been very careless?"

Henry sat up at that, for he felt sure that, whatever his sins, that was not one of them. Nevertheless he listened.

"You have been careless," she continued, "regarding the way you have used your attention. Day after day you have feared that your business would follow the course it did in the past, when almost every year you got into the red. Your thought was fixed anxiously on what had happened before and was thereby deflected from what to think and do in the present. This inevitably led to a deficiency as to how to design and plan for a better future. No wonder you broke down."

"What should I have done?" Henry asked, in much the same voice he had used while questioning his mother when he was in knee breeches.

"There are three right steps in good thinking," she told him, "all three of which you should use while planning, with the focus of your attention put firmly on how to design the sequences you erect. You should use your memory to help you to recall what succeeded in the past, how it was accomplished and why that way of doing was chosen. Failures are useful to help point out the mistakes. The successes of yesterday are guides to show you what to do today. That is the first step. Next comes your reason. The situations you have to deal with in the present may not be exactly like those you were troubled with in the past. You need to achieve logical conclusions. You need to establish by good judgment the correct procedures in the now, what is wise to do in order to be sure of the best results in the future. Reason helps you to apply statistics, analysis, comparison and perception as to how well the procedures that succeeded in the past will achieve in the present. While I was in the Department of Commerce I discovered again and again that business firms failed because they had not changed their ways to suit the times. That's the purpose of reason."

"O.K., what's next?" Henry was getting interested.

"Then you have a very good imagination," she continued.

"How do you know?" he broke in.

"Because if you didn't have it you couldn't have worried so much. Instead of using it to help you conceive the ways and needs of tomorrow, you made your imagination grovel as

157

an underling of anxiety. In our talk last week you showed me how you have imagined every sort of terrible consequence coming upon you and your business, and at the same time carelessly letting the sort of sequences develop that would surely bring those disasters to pass."

"Careless?" he pressed.

"Yes," she insisted, "that word seems to bother you, doesn't it? How much care in the month before you came here to rest had you put into the designing of good sequences? That means precise and definite strategies, such as a general would deliberate upon. How much care—yes, care—have you given to this determining of the cause—the correct cause—that will be sure to produce the desired results—as sure, that is, as life ever permits?"

"Very little, I guess."

"You guess? What do you know?"

"I know I worried, and got all messed up instead of . . ."

"So since there was no care where care was needed, you were careless, weren't you?"

"I guess so."

"You only guess so?"

"Damn it all—pardon me—yes, yes, yes, I was careless."

"Which," she said quietly, "is just why you are here in this sanitarium."

Let me repeat that all futures are created in the now. The best we can do in the present determines the results that will come to pass in the future. That is the secret of good fortune in everyday living. From our citadel of inner poise we gain social vision and learn how to do our work in relation to the world in which we are forced to live.

This is the fifteenth step in the achievement of poise.

16 EFFICIENT THOUGHT

O ESTABLISH sensory equivalents that are so true and right that we can thereafter surrender ourselves to their functional power and let them carry us is the greatest of all achievements.

To accomplish this constructive aim there is no thinking method as efficient as that which is called the *what-how-why-who-where-when* technique. These six words are the mightiest in all language, when connected into a practical process of thought. The efficiency of their union is invincible.

It is because most of your associates do not know how to think in this concrete way that they indulge in biased conclusions. There are quite a few morons in the world, but believe me there are millions of dormorons: people whose wits are asleep and who, because of the dormant state of their intellects, think and act like morons, and are resistant when you yourself use your intelligence. In the last analysis intelligence is an instinctive use of the what-how-why-who-where-when technique.

Does not a great and practical thinker first consider *what* it is his attention is focused upon? He studies the facts of substance, the combinations of material, the structure, and lists the phenomena that exist. Does he not then consider *how* that which he is concerned with operates, how it came into being, *how* it moves, grows, changes and has the motions that its combinations make possible? From seeing *what* a circle was, man next saw *how* it could operate when filled with an adequate substance so as to move over the surfaces of the ground. Thus a wheel came into being. Every *what* in nature and in scientific thought is followed by a *how*.

But a *how* is only a measure of motion with a hundred hidden uses unless man knows *why* the *whats* and the *hows* are what they are and function as they do.

The broadening of his practices depends on his comprehension of theories, and the laws and principles by which the theories are applied. From the discovery of the *whys* science was born. The physical world was thereby controlled. Subjective insight and formative penetration then reshape the objective plane of existence.

We are, however, not mere products of nature, living in a solitary forest or the aloneness of a desert. Humanity is gregarious. Thus it is that a science, when successfully concerned with geology, astronomy, chemistry, physics and the great field of cosmics, is always inadequate for a growing, surging humanity. *Who* is to use that which science discovers? *Who* is to operate the machines it makes possible? Is there not a need of development in man himself if mechanics and science are to endure and continually to serve? *Who* is to take part and *who* will be affected by man's cosmic consciousness and productive perception? To solve this enigma, sociology, philosophy and the great field of bionomics—the science of man as distinct from the world he lives in—became essential.

The thought processes of science, however, would never have been complete had the question of *where* been neglected. A cam may be so adjusted as to lift a valve in exactly the desired manner, and this is true of all operative parts. But where shall the cam be placed? Can you conceive any machine coming into being if the *wheres* were neglected? Could a great cathedral be built without the *wheres* being considered for every aspect of its structure? Even a military commander deploying troops, or the strategy in a business of sales promotion, requires careful consideration of the *wheres*.

Nor is this all, for time is an inevitable factor both of nature and of human nature. *When* is man's effort to be made and *when* can he use his expanded powers? Time is of the essence, a fourth dimension which, if ignored, compromises in serious ways the other three measurements of a material world. *When*, therefore, became as mighty a word in the vocabulary of science as any of the other five factors. Not a single machine could operate were there no timing of its motions. *When* shall an eccentric lift a valve? Must it not often be timed to a thousandth part of a second?

The thinking efficiency of any person—man or woman, bobbed-haired schoolgirl or tousle-headed boy—becomes multiplied many times by the use of the what-how-why-who-where-when technique. It can ease tension in one's work, in the home and even at contract bridge.

In any and every problem, separate each of these six elements from each other and study them apart from the other elements. Analyze the *whats* by themselves as factors with which you must deal. How did they come to pass? Why are they there? Who played a part in their existence? Where are these *whats* and where did they come from? When did they appear? This is the first step. It places the problem and reveals what it is.

The second step considers how one is to proceed, having achieved the preliminary clarification of the situation. How must he now act, and why? Who can he get to help him and where? When should he make the first move?

It is obvious one next asks oneself, "Why am I the one to do this? Who else is involved? Where is he, or are they? When could one expect to know which of the people or the forces concerned can be successfully dealt with?"

This what-how-why-who-where-when technique has many variations, and can be used in countless ways. The order of use is not rigid. A philosopher in his thought starts with the *whys*, following them by the *hows* until he reaches the *whats*. Until this concrete thinking has established a coherent series of answers, he is not concerned with the *whos, wheres,* or *whens*. A police officer or a detective, on the other hand, at once needs to discover the *whos, wheres* and *whens*. He does not consider the *whats, hows* and *whys* until he has made some progress in discovering the identities, the places and the times that are to be found in the situation with which he must deal. So important are the six aspects of this great technique that a lengthy book might be written about its use and the miracles in thinking it is capable of achieving.

When it comes to the more serious problems many of us need to strengthen the what-how-why-who-where-when process by a still more tangible means. This technique is called *the card method.*

For a great many years I have received credit for more intelligence than I possess. This is because of being able to solve what seemed to some people to be quite unsolvable problems. It was not my brains that unraveled the riddles but the use of the efficiency method of thinking.

I doubt if you could add 90871951784 and 139375827 in your head. I am sure you can do it quite easily on paper.

It is amazing to see how many people try to solve their problems in their heads. When they fail, they consider them to be unsolvable. They would not find the solutions difficult if they would do them in written form.

I personally use three-by-five filing cards because they are easier to handle and to move into various positions.

Time and again men and women have come to me with problems that had not only caused them worry but years of strain. They were often surprised at how promptly the enigma was clarified. I recall one case where a businessman brought me a problem that had absorbed the board of directors of his company for many months. We discussed the situation in a two-hour interview. When the next day I was able to give him the answer to his problem, he could hardly believe his ears.

Before coming to the solution of this man's problem I had written over two hundred cards—one factor, one idea only, on each card. Everything he had said to me as well as all I could remember or reason out had gone onto the cards. Then, using my whole office floor, I placed the cards in as logical a relation as I could imagine. But soon I was moving card after card into different positions and studying different combinations. I had to write new cards that the new relations suggested. How many millions of combinations of cards, of ideas, of facts and figures can be produced with two hundred cards, I do not know. I do know that not a human being has ever lived who could carry in his head the enlightenment of all the combinations I made in an evening. New insight on the problem did not result from each move. Understanding of the situation began to appear only after a series of placements.

Thus the first process in the use of the cards is called a free association method because one moves the cards spontaneously in response to whatever the chance combination suggests. It is always wise to let the cards reveal what they happen to show from unplanned arrangements before a controlled process is used. Having written down all that one has so far learned, the next step is to combine the card method with the what-how-why-who-where-when technique and to separate all the cards into six groups under the heading of these six key words. After this is done rearrange the cards into a logical order, keeping the six groups entirely separate. One need not always use so exhaustive a survey, but in such a serious case as I had to consider the full process was necessary.

Soon I was excitedly writing down the information that various combinations made evident. Before two hours of this card shifting and arrangements had elapsed, a starkly clear picture of the company's dilemma and the way out of it was before me. I could not in years have thought through such a complex business difficulty. The solution was certainly not created by me. The cards and the what-how-why-who-where-when process did it. This procedure has done it for me many times. Using this technique, a man of only reasonable intelligence can think out an intricate problem more easily than could a genius.

The card method is not limited to the clarifying of commercial difficulties. It is adjusted to all sorts of needs. For years I have used it to make the titles of books, articles and lectures. I write down on cards all possible words that might be in a title, one word on a card. Then I move the cards from position to position until the title appears. To the card method I also owe many of the contributions I have made to the field of psychology, but feeling that the cards did it I have never wished to claim credit for any advancement of our knowledge that may have resulted.

I know of no procedure that can more surely remove worry

and strain from one's work, if that work is more than manual. Even home, marriage and child-rearing problems are greatly clarified by use of this concrete system.

Whenever you cannot seem to think your way through a situation without exhaustion, use the cards. Write only one fact, one idea, one element of your problem on a single card, for you will need to be able to give any fact, idea or element a new context. This is the purpose of moving the cards about. Think deeply what each new context has to say to you, for in the new relation may be hidden a most significant message.

Suppose, for example, Mrs. Northly is upset about her boy's behavior. He is not doing well in school, and seems to have gotten in with a group of wild companions. Being in the "troublesome teens" he likes late hours, dances, girls and she knows not what else.

Let us suppose someone tells her about this efficient thinking process. So instead of lying sleepless in bed she takes up her filing cards and writes down all the facts she knows. These *whats* should not be limited to the mere elements of the present situation. They should include all she knows or can remember that might throw light on such a situation. She might recall that as a girl she was a bit wild herself, and also that the lad's father had been more so. Then come the facts that concern the boy's low grades. Let us suppose he is not a scholastic type, or at least does not fit readily into the present-day system. He is, let us say, in character, nature loving and yet rather mechanically inclined. He likes to use tools. The school he attends does not accent this type of study. It emphasizes Latin and the classics. A consideration of how the boy thinks reveals the fact that, being bored, her son is misfitted in his scholastic efforts. That is at least a start toward a true understanding of the situation. How is he conducting himself and how would he conduct himself if given more outlets for his native tendencies? Down on the cards go a whole series of enlightening activities, revealing hints of the way the problem may be solved.

Then come the *whys*. Why is her son acting as he does? Why is he so restless? Why has he gotten in with the some-what wild gang? Why do girls brook so large in his field of interest? Why haven't his parents before this seen that their son, who as a little boy played alone with tools in his work-shop, would rebel in one way or another when forced to study the classics? She admits to herself that Latin means no more to her boy than it did to her as a girl, or than the study of dynamic symmetry in the field of aesthetics would mean to his father. Had she not for twenty years tried to interest her husband in surrealism, and the work of the imagists in poetic expression, only to have him blink at her like a blind owl? And had she not wanted to curl up as if she had cramps in her stomach when her sports-minded husband wanted her to get excited over baseball scores and the latest type of flies to catch the wily trout? A sudden new compassion for her boy's dilemma comes over this surprised mother. Has she ever here-tofore understood her son?

Who then is involved in this situation? *She* certainly is, and so is his father, also the rigidities of the educational sys-tem in their town. Then there is little Millie Perkins to whom her boy seems so attracted. She is not a bad sort. And had not *she* herself been boy crazy in *her* teens? Wasn't it natural? Maybe Millie was a good influence!

For the first time in months Mrs. Northly begins to relax. She feels the strain oozing out of her, and a new sense of peace coming to pass. Since she seems to be getting help she keeps on with the cards. Who else is in this picture or could be? Well, several of the boys and one or two of the girls in her son's set might not be the best sort of companions at a time of such rebellion. Are there no other *whos* who might help? There is her brother Frank who operates a machine shop in a small Midwestern city. It is quite a long way from their own home, but might not Frank be a good influence on "Sonny"?

Mrs. Northly picks up some more cards, and begins to consider the *where* to which her boy might go. There is that new manual arts school that is being built in their neighboring city. Would it be wise to let Sonny go there? The *wheres* and the *whens* begin to work together. If her boy went to the new school, when would that be? Not until fall—after the summer vacation. Where could he go for the summer? Maybe to work in his uncle Frank's machine shop. And then to the school in the fall where they teach engineering. Mrs. Northly sighs. Why hadn't she thought of this solution before? She would have avoided so much strain.

The fact is that she hadn't thought of it before because she had not used an efficient thinking method. Instead she had indulged in what is technically called "circular brooding." Her mind had whirled around and around like a squirrel in a cage. She had never really stopped to deliberate on her son's problem. She had resisted the fact that he had outgrown his short pants and the simpler interests of his childhood. Feeling that he was becoming "another man," and hence a biological stranger to her, she had worried rebelliously and accomplished nothing but sleeplessness.

A slow, quizzical smile comes over Mrs. Northly's face. Can she ever convince her husband he isn't so smart but that the card method and the what-how-why-who-where-when technique could help him in his business? Lots of times she recalls he has shown how much strain his work produces. Is it possible he would be interested in using this new method? Or will he treat it as if it were "another of her fads"? Mrs. Northly wonders if he will listen. She recalls that men do not like to have a woman tell them anything, least of all how they might learn to think efficiently in business.

It must be apparent that in the use of the efficient thinking methods one is not so much using his own mind as he is following thinking processes that allow it to work for him. The card technique includes both the free and the controlled association processes, while the what-how-why-who-where-when procedure is only a vehicle into which intelligence spontaneously flows. Both are ways that work *for* one so that his own efforts are eased.

Those of us who have taught, lectured and written books on psychotherapeutic methods have long pondered as to why those who learn about the improved ways of living so seldom apply them. It is indeed discouraging to those of us who try to help the world to have to find so little use made of the great new means now available.

This neglect of the ways out of failure and strain is especially apparent when it comes to using the what-how-why-who-where-when method, either with or without the filing card technique. Personally, I have had the experience in my office practice of showing a client fully and clearly how I used this means of efficient thinking in solving some one of his or her problems. Again and again I have made it clear what he would gain if he developed the habit of using such a solver of riddles. Yet it has sometimes been years before my listeners have roused themselves out of the old habits of fumbling thought and begun to clarify their own conclusions by this simple, practical means.

It is from using this method until one becomes more and more familiar with it that its efficiency develops. It is by repetition that one acquires skill. It is from the success that one thereby achieves that a conviction as to what it can accomplish comes to pass.

No matter what your brains or how experienced you are in your daily tasks, this means of efficient thought can add great power to your intellectual accomplishment. The more you use it, the more people will come to think of you as a gifted individual. Many a genius thinks by this means but does so unconsciously. He does not know he is using such a method. He dropped into it as a way of achievement because of his genius. If he is egotistical, he may even think the results he is able to bring to pass are entirely because of his special brilliance. But it isn't so, any more than a man moving at fifty miles an hour in a motorcar has a "self" that makes him able to go that fast. It is not his body or his mind. It is the instrument he possesses that endows the power.

The use of these techniques of efficient thinking is an essential concrete step in the art of constructive living. They open the door to life and show how the application of creative methods is achieved.

Learning to think in an ever more orderly way is the sixteenth step in the art of easing out of strain.

17 CONSTRUCTIVE AUTOMATISM

*I*T SEEMS not to occur to the average person that the scientific advances that have so transformed the world resulted from an amazing union of laziness and discontent on the one hand, and of research and initiative on the other. Had man been willing to toil with his hands from sunrise to nightfall, he would never have invented the great machines that now do so much of his work. Were he not weary of living by the sweat of his body he would not have produced the means to avoid it. All over the world man is seeking so to understand the laws of nature that, by using them in objective ways, he may make easier the work that must be done.

So many are these mighty cosmic principles, it takes great tomes to explain them. But a knowledge of all of them is not essential to successful adjustment in a mechanical age. There are, however, two basic factors we must understand if we are by sensory equivalents, or by any other means, to make the best usc of available knowledge: these are momentum and automatism. One of the aspects of laziness and discontent is that somewhere in the depths of our natures we *know* that there is a spontaneous way to do things. We sense how momentum may carry us forward without the old humdrum effort.

Have you ever watched a good driver handling his car as he approaches a hill? He does not slow down to shift gears unless the hill is abnormally steep. He puts on more power and depends upon the momentum of his car to carry it over the top.

Have you ever tried to start a cold car on a frosty morning? It may start and then stop time and time again, but after you have "got it running" the momentum which the engine has established carries it through the hard places that at first caused the machinery to stall.

Have you ever watched any sort of engine in operation? Momentum is one of the secrets of its motion. It carries it forward until the next release of power gives it another shove.

Few people realize the importance of momentum, and many have never established it in their lives. Lacking it, every effort has to start with no impetus as if only beginnings were important. What *has* been done, however, will greatly ease what *can* be done, if one's momentums are of a constructive nature. Which means, of course, that we should make sensory equivalents of the way our minds can develop momentums just as such automations permit machincs to function.

Providing it is in good order, mechanical equipment acts according to its nature. You push a button and a motor begins to whirl. Its response is spontaneous because its nature is created to do a certain work. More than this, it continues to function as long as the fuel lasts and the machine remains in order. It possesses a capacity for automatism. But you must start it going by some compulsive means.

Beyond all man-made contrivances the human mind possesses the powers of spontaneous response, of automatic functioning. Were this not so human beings would long ago have worn
out. Great operational patterns become established in the mind
that do their work without continued effort. There is no finer
gift, nor one more ignored and misused, than the spontaneous
automatic momentums of the human intellect once a definite
action pattern has set it in motion.

Just at the present moment you are using the most common
of all spontaneous automatic momentums. Your eyes are
deciphering the words on the page of this book. The printed
letters have formed an equivalent of the thought you seek to
know. The print is a spontaneous starter of the assimilation
process. You are not in the least concerned with the act of
reading; that is taking care of itself. You are busy thinking,
weighing and measuring my thought. The act of reading is a
spontaneous automatic momentum that moves on and on in
so effortless a way that you are hardly aware you are doing
anything. Were you a boy absorbed in an adventure story,
or a girl lost in a romantic novel, you would not even be present, as it were, but compellingly *in* the adventure or the novel,
and in a sense not even in the room where you were sitting.

In reading you have an example of the way you can and
ought to do everything you do in life. Work done in this way
creates little or no fatigue and produces infinitely better results.
It can be mastered as a way of life. Nor is there any gift so
great or any way one's intellectual power can so expand as by
the art of spontaneous automatic momentum. It is not only
the secret of genius but when instigated by sensory equivalents
it is the one way to enduring power. It is also true that, once
established, this great mental process takes over and needs
no further attention.

One of the saddest mistakes made in the whole field of

clinical psychology is to suppose one must continue to make the same conscious effort that his first striving to master a technique requires. Nothing could be further from the fact. We are, as I have already written, creatures of habit and habits once established function automatically. Even though it may not be your native tongue, perhaps you have learned to speak French. You may think in it easily and the idioms that were once so hard are used unconsciously. This gift and the principle by which it functions is the basis and means of intellectual automatism.

Momentum is a priceless possession, and one of the greatest easers of strain. It comes from consecutive use of purpose, in patterns suited to the same task and with an aim in one direction. Concentration is the key to conquest, conservation of energy its purpose, and continued effort the producer of confidence. "Let's get the ball rolling."

Life will either carry you or you must carry it. Make your choice. If you don't want to be loaded down by a hundred requirements put upon you by every self-indulgent person in your community—more skillful at working others than at working himself—stop now and decide on a few essential values or activities of your life. Decide to concentrate on those momentum patterns, and do so so intensely that you won't even hear the cry of the parasites wishing to get upon your back. They may become irritated because your back is no longer available. But what of it! You can become so busy planning on how you will do the things that belong to you to do that a pertinent respect for you grows up in your would-be detractors. Then like a calm river the momentum of your interests sweeps you along with a steady flow, and most of the old strain which came from always having to begin is gone.

What you have done is only part of what you can continue to do, and those who are constant doers never need to talk about why they have done what they have done. It is an inherent part of what they are still doing. They do what they do with ease because they are carried along by a momentum from the past through the present into the future.

Much tush is being taught and preached as to the value of work, as if it had for its own sake any merit at all. Maybe the devil finds mischief for idle fingers, but he extracts crime from tired brains. It is not work that has value but the discovery of an interest it becomes one's work to fulfill. "Occupation is the armor of the soul," wrote Hilliard. Did he not know it has also, when it is mere toil, taken from the soul all hope, all health and all happiness? It is not occupation, as such, that is important but how we are occupied. "Blessed is he who has found *his* work," wrote Carlyle, "let him ask no other blessedness." When a man is admonished to put his heart into a work that is not his, he is not blessed but damned. What he does with interest must fulfill some hope and express some ruling love or his toil is a torture.

On the other hand, occupation when it is a way of fulfilling the surge of a man's being is blessed indeed. One cannot then, as Baron said it, have any time for tears. Work also becomes, to quote Leigh Hunt, "the necessary basis of all enjoyment."

It is an enthusiasm for what we do, not a duty, that arouses in us that spirit of greatness of which Goethe spoke so powerfully when he wrote: "Be always resolute with the present. Every moment is of infinite value for it is the representative of eternity." How different this attitude wherein toil becomes a majesty, from the drudgery of enforced duty. When interest rules, the latent genius that is in every man is released to do its own striving. "Every man who observes vigilantly and resolves steadfastly grows unconsciously into genius," wrote Bulwer-Lytton.

174

It is in any case our privilege to analyze the ways of genius that in finding its secrets we may ourselves avoid the idiocies of the commonplace. Can we not believe with Longerius that "the sublime, when it is introduced at a seasonable moment, has often carried all before it with the rapidity of lightning and shown at a glance the mightiest power"? Let us cease to put genius on one plane and humanity on another, for as Hamilton Mabie tells us: "It is intensity of life, an overflowing vitality which floods and fertilizes a continent or a hemisphere of being, which makes a nature many sided and whole, while most men remain partial and fragmentary."

Must we remain partial and fragmentary? If by the use of the techniques that conserve one's strength and give one many times more power we cease to devitalize ourselves, may we not also come to possess an "overflowing vitality which floods and fertilizes"? In this reference Bulwer-Lytton gives us a mighty warning. He tells us a man of genius is inexhaustible only in proportion as he always nourishes his "genius." Do we not become exhausted in the same way, and to an even greater degree? And would we not, if we insistently nourished what genius we have, come far closer to possessing it in actuality and in sufficient measure to let us live invincibly?

The trouble is we have been taught to be plow horses and from infancy everyone has tried to tame us. Oliver Wendell Holmes said: "Genius is always impatient of its harness: its wild blood makes it hard to train." Let us be impatient then, for our blood is just as wild. Nor is there any reason to suppose that if it were set free we would riot. "The true characteristic of genius," wrote Channing, is that "without despising rules it knows when and how to break them." That is not a lost art nor need we be afraid to learn it. "Genius does not care much for a set of explicit regulations," Lewes insists; and then he wisely adds, "but that does not mean that genius is lawless." It merely, as Willmot said, "finds its own road and carries its own lamp."

Much that is true has been thought and spoken by the great of earth as to how they achieved and maintained their greatness. There is a major point, however, which all of them seem to have missed, and that is to explain the way a mind works to produce the achievement that can be called the product of genius. Years of research as to what the genius knew about himself and his own mental processes fails to reveal that he had any actual insight as to what so empowered his genius as to make it what it was. Those endowed with genius seemed to have known little or nothing about the intellectual automation that, like a mighty machine, reduces toil, time and trial to a minimum. Nor had they any true understanding of an association process that makes this magic possible.

There are many ways in which the activities of human thought and those of engineering are kindred, none more startling than this gift of association. No machine will work unless the parts are properly put together. Design is essential to the establishment of any permanent structure. Once the right principles are obeyed and the cams, levers, rods and chambers are constructed, an engine produces power for other instruments to use. All machines are made possible by the act of connecting the various attributes. Once organized into units of structure, momentum of one kind or another functions within their relationships to produce automatic response.

As with the human mind and in the construction of and use of machinery, automatic momentum is a great means for easing us out of strain. Intellectual automatism is, in fact, the mighty way we can avoid the tension of unabated effort. We have thought structures, feeling tones and action patterns latent within us that will rise as responses to stimulus when needed.

A person who sees how mechanical procedures have eased

and yet increased the power of the industrial world should gain a conviction that this same benefit can develop in the handling of his own nature. Those who believe this fact, and believing it strive to live that way, are the ones who grow more and more into the genius level and possess its gift. It is they who are willing to make effort to acquire the techniques that will later operate spontaneously. This preliminary attention does not add to a person's toil in life. It reduces it, for after one learns to depend upon automatism most of his work is done in an effortless way. He makes his only striving when establishing the procedures.

Without the association process human beings could have no coherent thought. Upon its action memory entirely depends, just as upon the interconnection of parts in a logical and workable manner the capacity of a machine depends. So upon the continuity and contiguity of the parts of thought its successful existence subsists. Nor is this all. But for the association process your five senses would be valueless. What you see, hear, touch, taste and smell would have no meaning for you if you did not possess a means by which the sensory vibrations become associated with the information of previous observations and thus are realized for what they are.

The first time a baby sees an orange he has no way of distinguishing it from a colored ball. Later on, having tasted the orange, he associates the taste with his sight and comes more and more fully to know by association what an orange is. The relation is made automatically. It requires not the least effort on the child's part to recognize an orange once the connection is established. There are countless such contiguities in the human mind of wonderful efficiency.

There is more to the association process than this, however, for it not only makes possible an interpretation of all sensory phenomena, while also endowing the capacity to remember,

177

but upon it that greatest of all mental attributes, automatism, depends. Each of the countless skills and habits that you now have is made possible by the power to associate. Nor is any phase of personal development more important than to establish association between ourselves and all we could wish to do. Functional paths, which we might call habituated automatisms, will then bring to pass the accomplishment we desire.

It is safe to say that but for the association process human beings could not live at all in such a speeded-up social order as our mechanical age has created. It is, moreover, just because millions have remained ignorant of what this great procedure can do for them that we still live in an unbalanced world. Not until everyone learns to live without strain, from a skillful development of associated momentums, can we hope to achieve a social equilibrium.

The organization of one's whole personal dynamic is brought into being by the use of the association process. It functions as a reminding process that unifies one's various endowments and fits the attributes of one's mind together.

All skills result from a union of the various capacities possessed by living creatures. You must have seen a sea gull gliding gracefully in the wind, adjusting itself to every gust with swift response. The art of its flight is made possible by the association process. You have listened to a great violinist and watched the superb adjustments of his hands to the dynamics of the music. His majestic responsiveness to its rhythm and harmony depends upon this same procedure. You have marveled at the flow of words when a lecturer is speaking. Not only is the language suited to the thought, but the voice, the emotional modulations, the sensory emphasis that make you live in his portrayal are all woven together with as intricate a skill as nature herself achieves. Such a capacity is made possible by this spontaneous automatism.

178

The strainless achievement that such a union of skills makes available is surely a true way to health and happiness. It is also a means of greatly increasing one's power. This method of relating one's mental attributes can, by a little conscious effort, multiply a person's capacity many times. It is established by persistent repetition and made permanent when equivalents are firmly established.

You automatically shake hands with your right hand rather than with your left. You have associated such a greeting with right-handedness. The association takes care of what you do. Often you aren't even aware of your act.

The uses of association as a means of self-command are limitless, but its greatest value lies, as we have said, in the automatic responses it makes available. A repeated association between any two relatable attributes of personality soon becomes so habituated in a pattern of equivalents that a spontaneous action results. You do not have to make effort to translate into thoughts and ideas the last conversation that took place in your life. The procedure is completely automatic. Your ears hear the words, and the thoughts in your mind respond so swiftly you are not conscious of a time span.

The same process makes possible the equivalents of thought of many of your life activities. Once fully learned, an invisible bond is established between any certain stimulus and a definite response. By developing and using this great means of spontaneous activity in all of a person's life it becomes greatly empowered and amazingly eased. One is no longer the victim of routine toil or perpetual strain but free to live his life dynamically.

Learning to impress our minds with the new and efficient ways so that we use them spontaneously in our efforts, and almost without knowing we do so, is the seventeenth concrete step in the art of creative living.

18 THINKING WITHOUT TENSION

$\mathcal{M}$ ost people know that from an application of the constructive automatism we have been discussing a revolution in the field of mechanics is taking place. It is changing the industrial life of all civilized lands. In engineering it is called *automation*. This is a technique by which various engineering processes do intricate tasks without human guidance. Machines of all sorts act with an almost superhuman intelligence. Wires, tapes, templets, eccentrics, rocker arms, jacquards, as well as the more recently developed electronic circuits, play their part in this miracle by which automation does our work. Mankind is at last learning nature's secret: that interrelated design is the one great constructive means and the key to the universe.

Most of us are aware of how these mechanical genii in industry produce lower costs, make better products, a wider use of conveniences and a steadier enjoyment for everyone. We know that these instruments with their air valves, pressure pumps, slide sockets, electric switches and "eyes," are constantly transforming our world. We see that when the stimulus, to which they are planned to respond, is put before them they do their tasks "spontaneously."

A hundred and fifty years ago one man with backbreaking toil could weave about three yards of the simplest cloth in a day. When the material was of fine quality, one yard was all he could produce. All kinds of fabrics are now woven by automation, and a day's product goes into figures almost too high to estimate. Before this book is printed the amount may be doubled or even trebled.

Automation developed because of the gradual command of interaction, knowledge of which was made possible by the research of modern science. Such laws as momentum and repetition made automation available to man. Some of the procedures depend upon timing, others on the exact shape of some moving part, many on the attributes of matter that are involved.

This great engineering technique functions through the use of structural principles. Its activities are made possible by the interrelation of processes and the variations of material. These differences are created by the designs of vibration of which substance is composed. They are manifestations in various densities, intensities and frequencies of the electromagnetism which is the basic element of matter. Every aspect of existence has certain quantities, qualities, strengths or endurances, and each is of a certain type or variety. In obedience to cosmic laws all of these attributes can be so related to other attributes as to bring into being a series of interconnected automatic operations.

In engineering, whenever any switch, eccentric, belt or other device comes into play, according to the relation of parts and the timing of their action, automation results. There must, however, be a balance between timing and structure, a rhythm of operation and a harmony between the procedures for automation to take place.

We, if we will, can learn from automation how our own lives can be so put in order that we too achieve this almost effortless way of living.

Not all parts of any machine or any manufacturing process are automatic. Some are merely sustaining. Some are static. True automation comes to pass only where a valve, an eccentric, a switch or some other part starts a repetitive process as cosmic as that of a pendulum in motion.

There are in our lives many places where we can establish repetitive processes so that we are set free of constant attention to what must be done. Our work is then achieved *through* us but not *by* us.

We set up what is called an association linkage by repetitive effort and momentum. We are far too accustomed to ignore the impelling of our endowments and so do not let them work for us. We tend rather in a sort of panic to rush into effort egotistically and without first connecting what we do with our inner powers. Multitudes of people live in this nervous haste all their lives, and die with their heritage of spiritual strength unused.

Each time we hear of how automation is releasing mankind from monotonous routine, let us remember that it is more than a commercial art. Must we observe it merely in the fields of manufacture and continue to ignore the fact that it has its place in the operation of that most intricate machine of all: the human mind? Should we not realize that it can do as much for us to ease us out of strain as it is doing for industry?

All attributes of life, as we have repeatedly said, depend first of all upon design, which is the principle of principles. Whoever comes to understand the importance of this great process and uses it in advance of effort of every kind transforms his whole relation to life and experience.

Let me repeat that no automatic machine is ever invented except in obedience to cosmic laws carried out into definitely planned structures. But no automation is ever a complete process. Just as the human body, itself the most amazing example of automation, requires a soul, so there must be an operator with various assistants to care for and direct any type of automation. This is a fact we should not forget.

Perhaps I will jolt one of the prejudices to which you may still hold by again condemning the value of hard, conscious effort. Such toil belongs to the days of the hand loom. I may further seem to conflict with what may be one of your biases by saying that the rebellion of a so-called lazy schoolboy is often right and justified. He is revolting against the adult delusion that a grim concentration in the act of study is the only way to acquire knowledge. The truth is that if learning is hard, the right method is not being used.

If your boy is failing in school it is because the educational system is failing him, not because he is failing the school. To learn is easy even for a moron if, but only if, the means nature created by which we may learn is followed and not the stuffing-in process that is substituted for it. I have personally had the experience in a large academy of teaching the twenty boys with the lowest grades how to think. Twelve rose to the honor list.

Thank God, it has not yet occurred to most parents that it is hard for a child to learn the language of his country. He is still allowed to acquire it spontaneously and with little effort. Its use is an automation. That he has many other native capacities that are quite as susceptible to unconscious habituation is seldom realized. Were he allowed to discover them instead of having hard effort forced upon him as discipline, his mind would open up to knowledge even as a flower blooms

183

obediently to the guidances of nature. Few, however, have had the privilege of natural development. With most people their teachers and parents were certain to believe they knew better than God as to how their child should be taught and what it should learn.

Nevertheless, even if your own parents taught you to make the act of living hard, and the doing of its tasks a difficult and self-conscious procedure, you can now as an adult become more and more interested in the automation that is going on in industry. You can, if you will, open your mind to the idea that the human brain can follow this principle quite as completely as the non-vital substances man must use to erect his automatic machines.

Once you get your egotism out of the way, you come to reverence how your power of imagery will work for you. You do not have to make it work. You merely turn your attention toward it as you would a motion picture and watch it function for you.

If you keep from tinkering with your imagination and subdue your intellectual pride, your creative gift will co-operate in an amazing way with your association process, reproducing for you in visual, auditory and tactile form what you have seen, heard and touched in the past. It will then make new combinations by putting parts of what you recall into new relation. This done, a true creative activity follows. Origination appears spontaneously. Invention comes into being, and that which never was before begins to appear. Lastly, this foresight induces the meaning, the use, the purpose of that which it has fabricated. A new understanding develops in preparation for an adjusted use of your thought.

If allowed to do so, just such a self-propelling activity takes place within every attribute of the mind. The child remembers because it does not try to do so. We, by making effort, force ourselves to forget. Did we not precipitate this tension, a free association process would work for us quite as unsupervised as does a great plant built to use automation. Our brains would then turn this free-flowing thought into a controlled form, for spontaneous mental effort is no less precise than are the activities of a modern factory.

It is one thing, however, to be told how wonderfully personal automation can ease you out of strain, quite another to achieve it unless you come to believe in it and hence to want it. The same type of scientific research that brought our mechanical age to pass has, most fortunately, also shown us that from wanting it it begins automatically to develop. We know at long last that a willingness to make effort to avoid effort shows the old disciplines of toil to be antiquated indeed. Even when you use a means of acquiring automation, you are only releasing an innate knowing that is already within you, even as it is inherent in all that lives.

Indeed, it is not too much to say that for all its electric eyes, wire banks, computation centers, switches, levers and cams, mechanical automation is a complicated and clumsy device in contrast to the inherent automatism of nature. Nor are our heavy and self-conscious attempts to discover those guidances we call knowledge and wisdom to be compared with the simple awareness of what to do and how to function successfully possessed even by an insect.

Sit in the summer by a little pond. Presently a queer brown bug crawls out of the water and climbs the swamp grass along the shore. It has never in all its life been out of the water before. The sunshine dries its shell. Soon a crack forms along its back. The shell opens and out crawls a bright blue zephyrous creature. It sits for a while higher up the blade of grass. As the sun dries its wings, they spread out in the soft summer air. Gracefully this amazing, living thing lifts its legs to be sure the

185

thin, iridescent fabric of its wings is fully stretched. Then, suddenly, it takes off above the pool, zigging and zagging as it searches for its natural food. It has never eaten such prey before. It has never until that moment flown. Its aeronautic skill is greater and more perfect than any aviator acquires from years of practice.

Many are the insects that follow this general pattern. Even the ubiquitous mosquito, who persistently flits about your head, was once a little water wiggler. Who taught it to fly so skillfully that it adroitly dodges the grasp of your hand? How does it know that you have red blood in your veins that will satisfy its appetite? And by what miracle is a little black, worm-like semifish transformed into a creature whose wings are so delicately transparent?

That a mosquito knows automatically how to fly is in itself one of the greatest evidences of inherent wisdom in living things. *Do we not possess within us such magnificent guidances?* Has nature endowed all other creatures with this most precious of information and neglected man—supposed to be the greatest of her accomplishments?

Have you ever given thought to the automatism of nature? Have you faced squarely the facts of the wisdom that inheres in the life around us? Have you stopped in the mad, sophisticated rush of modern intellectualism to ask yourself if there is any way that we too can receive automatically and without effort wisdom of what to do, how to live and why each choice of activity is made? Is it not possible that the same senses inhere in us, innate but neglected? May it not be that without some per cent of such guidance, equivalent to and perhaps greater than that possessed by any other living creature, man in his prehistoric days could not have survived?

Who told him what plants were good to eat and what were poisonous? What were the means by which he learned the lore that helped him to conquer the earth? Most of all, how did the miracle of language come to pass by which he informed his fellows of what he knew?

These are thoughts that are important to us in this over-speeded, mechanized world. If we too are to survive, a means of knowledge deeper than that of the facts of materialism must be ours. There should be some way back to what Robert Browning called "Those manifold possessions of the brute, gained most as we did best."

There is.

We have already seen how majestically valuable the association process is, and that it is the means that makes automatic thought, emotion and activity possible. We know that it is the ability that endows man's mind with what is equivalent to automation in industry. We have seen that by repetition great expression ways are established in consciousness. We know that through these habits, and by means of them, we are able to carry on most of the activities of life without the effort and the delay of conscious intent. We see that this is all made possible by the interconnective action of association.

Impressive as this endowment is, however, it is not the greatest capacity of the mind; for we also possess the ability to let it act for us as a receiver of just such guidances as endow other living creatures with their instinctive and protective knowledge.

But let us at this moment pause and ask ourselves the question: if we have in our brain such a capacity, why do we not use it as easily as do the insects, fish, beasts and birds? History tells us that man has neglected many essential facts of life and of his own nature. The knowledge that has been lost because of wars, and from a hundred other causes, is great indeed. But no loss is so serious as that of the ancient wisdoms as to the operation of the human mind. The lore of Egypt and

187

the culture of Greece were but remnants of this once superb understanding of self-use and self-mastery. All we have left is an awareness that the association process is an instrument with two distinct attributes: one that is controlled in type, and one that is free.

Man's conscious power to remember and to reason logically concerning what he recalls is made possible by controlled association. This is the ability that makes us able deliberately to connect our knowledge with the various attributes of life. The assemblage of knowledge and most that we call education depends upon this guided capacity.

Free association, on the other hand, is a very different process, akin to the means by which an insect learns how to fly. It is the gift that makes inspiration possible. It is the procedure upon which instinct depends. Without it we would have no capacity for prescience. In the last analysis it is the secret of intelligence.

You have only to resort to your dictionary to realize that intelligence is the ability to know what to do, how to act and why a situation is what it is, even if you have never come in contact with that experience before. The intellect depends upon knowledge previously acquired. Intelligence may use such information, but it does not depend upon it. Rather is there a guidance at work when intelligence functions that is not unlike the knowledge of how to act that is possessed by the other members of the animal kingdom. There is what is equivalent to inherent wisdom as to how to proceed, why the new situation is what it is and what to do to deal with it efficiently.

Intelligence, then, is a true automation, an organization of all the spontaneous powers of the mind, but it is most distinctly still dependent upon the association process, albeit that of a free type.

When you sit down to think quietly by yourself, you do not always resort to logical reason. Much of your thinking is free floating. You are not directing your thought. It seems rather to have its own purposes. It is carried by its own momentum. You are not always aware of thinking at all. Your sight plays with this and that object about you. Your hearing receives impressions to which you pay no conscious attention. Your sense of touch may come into the procedure.

In any case, your mind with its gift of imagination is actively engaged in this "brooding." Then suddenly a constructive thought pops up. You have an intuition, or maybe it is an inspiration. It could even seem like an act of clairvoyance or clairaudience. At least, you *see* something you never saw before. You *feel* a truth you had in the past but dimly realized. You *know* a fact that was hitherto a doubt.

We each have had such experiences, but most people do not sense that they were at such a time exhibiting a remnant of what was once man's greatest power. Nor do they realize that this gift can be recovered gradually by the use of modern therapies. Each and all of the methods help. It must be evident that advanced effort directly conduces to an automatic reception of knowledge. It should be clear that visual imagery is a means of developing ever greater capacity to clarify and to functionalize one's thought. Induced autosuggestion is also a means of establishing this automation in place of the laborious and conscious-minded habits of mere reasoning.

All of these therapies are then put into constructive practice by the actuation process, and by this procedure the sensory equivalents become habits and effortless thinking is brought back to the individual.

But we should never for a moment suppose that by these means we create the capacities we then use. They are not *made by us*. They are innate. They are at long last being *used*.

189

Our attitude toward them should be one of gratitude. We should reverence the fact that we possess them. It is this spirit of appreciation that stimulates them into action. From a belief that their activity is natural comes a respect that helps them to function without self-conscious interference with their expression.

Have you ever watched an eagle sitting speculatively on a treetop? He may not be able to do calculus but he is not devoid of the gift of calculation. As he sits he observes. His alert eyes take in the whole scene. He perceives the various facts and these he obviously organizes into a single concept. Upon that conclusion he acts.

Have you ever watched a fox using his wits? He is not so skilled in surveying a situation as is an eagle, but at analysis he is a master. He sits quietly to observe the behavior of a rabbit. He is silently taking apart the situation, studying the significance of each motion of his prey. After a while his judgment tells him what the animal upon whom he is concentrated will do. He then moves to the appropriate position to "fox" his prey.

Perhaps you know dogs: those with good blood and also those wonderful creatures whose mothers made "an awkward step." Not all curs are brilliant, of course, but neither are all thoroughbreds. When either is, and has a master who loves him and allows him to show his powers, these canine geniuses will sometimes exhibit a masterly sense of comparison. It is as if a spontaneous reasoning worked in them, as if one fact related itself to another fact and the result to a third and then a fourth attribute of a situation until an impelling automation is set in motion. The dog then rushes off to save someone's life or to do some other incredible deed.

Years ago, in Switzerland, I crossed the Theodule Pass. A furious blizzard came suddenly upon us. This vast stretch of ice and snow lies between the Matterhorn and the Breithorn. In clear weather it is not a difficult ascent, but if a blinding storm hits you after you have left the lower hut, your life is in danger.

After weary hours of climbing, our guides admitted that the snow was so heavy they did not know where we were. Another party that was near us at the start had disappeared. All was an endless waste of white, above, below and about us. We might for all we knew be headed for the crevasses at the base of the Breithorn, and far to the left of our true trail. Then out of the ever falling snow came a Saint Bernard dog. He wasted no time, but at once grabbed hold of the upper end of our rope and, moving backward, began to pull. Not once did he turn around to see where he was going. He backed up all the way to the upper hut.

How did he know his way through the howling blizzard with its bitter cold? I do not know. That it was a dangerous storm is testified to by the fact that another dog who found the other party had to search for them far off the normal line of ascent. He located them and brought them to the hut, but too late for one of the men. His legs had frozen and had to be amputated when they got him to a hospital.

The details of this experience are not, of course, important, but the fact of that great dog's sensory wisdom is. May I mildly suggest I have more reverence for it than might have been the case had I not been caught in a blizzard on the Theodule? I am still more in awe of it, however, when men and women reveal this gift, and merge it with all the other means of spontaneous conclusion.

A preliminary merging of the therapies into the momentum of a personal automation is the eighteenth step in the art of conquering strain.

19   YOU ARE NOT YOUR MIND

*I*F THE radio had been in active use before William
James passed into the life beyond, he would have
been the first to use it as guidance in the establishment of new
ways. James created the significant phrase "the will to believe,"
which gives one faith in the existence of powers beyond those
already evident at a given time. There is nothing mystical or
impractical about the will to believe. It is not an abstruse or
an occult activity. It is founded on common sense.

We possess today countless achievements of modern civilization that were not even thought of a century ago. During the
war of 1812 my great-grandfather drove my grandmother ten
miles in an old surrey on an ancient dirt road to watch the
burning of Portland, Maine, which had been set afire by the
British soldiers. I am sure it was a slow and arduous journey.
I doubt if either of these forebears of mine dreamed of the
fine cement road, or the powerful motorcar in which I last
made that same journey.

The will to believe is an attitude that enables one to look

forward to better things while still destined to use those things that then exist. A slow-moving, horse-drawn surrey is not efficient, nor a rutted dirt road a successful highway. The will to believe looks ahead to consider how the road and the vehicle can be improved.

William James knew that if one had the will to believe he tapped "hidden energies" and thus more easily accomplished his purposes. He taught that one also felt such confidence in the process that he relaxed and let the guidance flow through him. The belief helped bring the better experience to pass.

It was his faith in this process that would have impelled James to use radio as a symbol of the way one could tap the inner wisdoms that are merged with the hidden energies. In the last analysis, the two aspects of inner power are one, for energy is of no use, and might be of some harm, without the wisdom of how to apply it.

In my introduction I mentioned the fact that James told me to "listen to my mind." He believed that we all possess hidden depths of intelligent and guiding instinct that we are prone to neglect. He would have us listen to the voices of these inner powers in just the way we listen to radio. He believed, moreover, that we are not deprived of the instinctive guidances that direct the lives of the animal kingdom. After using the example of the wonderful homing instinct of the carrier pigeon, he remarked to a group of startled listeners, "I know you fellows act as if you are less than pigeons, but are you?"

That is a mighty question. Are you willing to maintain that you are less than a pigeon and do not possess its instinctive power of guidance? Are you without the gift that directs a salmon back to the stream of its birth, or the innate skill that makes it unnecessary for an insect to be taught how to fly? Let us go further, for mankind has demonstrated gifts of inventive thought that have conquered the earth itself and far outstrip the abilities of the birds and the bees, the fish and the beasts of woods and fields. Yet few have the will to believe that they have boundless hidden energies and untapped intelligence in their hidden depths. Had they this "will to believe," no example would then be more important to follow than that of radio. One would then "listen to his mind" as attentively as one listens to a broadcast and thereby begin to balance one's relation to the imbalanced world in which one toils.

In Hamlet's speech to the players he gave us memorable wisdom: "O'erstep not the modesty of nature . . . but suit the action to the word and the word to the action." We might well paraphrase this advice by saying: Suit what you think, say and do to the situations with which you have to deal.

There is no question that when all the theories as to the art of living are reduced to simple form, successful adaptations that are also correct adjustments are found to be the center of each of them. Applications are not made in space. Good ideas are valueless if hung on the clouds.

The best of all aphorisms are but idle words if we are not shown how to use them. Nor is there any greater waste of time than to peruse the moral verbiage of recent centuries that told us to hitch our wagons to a star. They gave us not the least knowledge as to how we might get there in all eternity. Mechanical idealism, with its painfully petty platitudes, has glutted man's consciousness until he has become drugged with virtues as gaping as a row of empty caskets.

It is not admonition but information we need. It is not manners but methods that will meet the problems of our days. We must know who we are and how to adjust to life without undue compromise.

There is no way to achieve this goal without a successful use of one's mind. What we do should depend on how we think. There are no perfect answers to our queries. It is the best that is possible we seek, not a solution so ineffable that it cannot accomplish anything.

Not even the greatest military genius who ever lived could design a strategy that would kill none of his soldiers. It is the least loss that such a man seeks. It is the surest encompassing of the enemy that is his aim. His must be a practical idealism, not a vapid virtue, or too many of his men will die. Thus it is how he thinks, what he thinks about and why his decision must be made that is all-important.

In 1945, some weeks after the Allied troops landed on the Normandy coast, I was asked to speak in the New York Town Hall, on how we might adjust successfully to the pressures of modern life. During my address, I explained that it is important to know how to use and relate memory, reason and imagination in the way we have discussed it in preceding chapters. By way of illustration, I used what I had concluded to be the means by which General Eisenhower (with the aid of his staff) had thought out and developed an efficient strategy long before he let our soldiers become exposed to the risk of landing on soil controlled by the enemy.

He and his advisers had, I affirmed, first resorted to the use of the association process. By recalling and studying many of the great campaigns of the past, important wisdom as to how then to proceed would come to light. I pictured these strategists as studying and explaining why this or that move had proved successful. Memory, I declared, always deals with the past, reason with the present, while imagination helps us to penetrate into the future. Thus it seemed probable, I said, that having discussed the techniques of many past campaigns, the Allied Staff would then turn to the use of reason. Logical calculations would alone make them able to decide what methods previously used were applicable to the threatening present that stood so starkly before them.

In an age of tanks, cavalry would be no longer used. Airplanes had come to transform many of the old maneuvers. Modern landing craft and submarines would greatly modify the approach to beachheads. Modern guns, capable of firing to great distances, had made possible the use of a covering barrage that was not at the disposal of the generals of even the preceding century.

Again I pictured General Eisenhower and his staff questioning, discussing, considering this plan, refusing that maneuver that once might have been wise. The skills of the past were not thereby ignored or refused, but remodeled and developed by the use of reason into methods adapted to the situation which had to be dealt with.

This use of logical calculation having been covered, I pictured the discussion that might have taken place from an application of imagination to the shifting situations that would certainly come about in so mobile and intense a war. How would the enemy change his plans, regrouping tanks here or there as the flux of battle swung back and forth? In what way would fleets of airplanes be deployed because of changing conditions? Where would the enemy make his stand, supposing that the Allied strategy had sent long tank raids, deeply penetrating his lines?

These and scores of other considerations could only be met beforehand by the use of each and every form of imagination. It must be definitely reproductive, so that what was thought out was as functional as an actual operation. It must be constructive, so that concrete embodiments of strategies could develop from the forethought. It must be interpretive, so that the staff could foresee the meaning of possible enemy moves. It must be creative, so that a kind of prophetic flexibility was quickly invented.

Only by such a dynamic use of imagination could a complete strategic campaign be developed.

Following this hypothetical analysis of the supposed discussions of General Eisenhower and his staff, I went on to say that this coherent relation of memory, reason and imagination was the truest and best way of thinking about any problem that came before us in everyday life.

After the question period was over, a man in uniform joined the group that is always eager to shake a speaker's hand. There was nothing perfunctory, however, in his warm grasp. "I want to tell you," he said in a strong, hearty voice, "that I was on General Eisenhower's staff at the time the discussions you so well described took place. You gave an almost perfect picture of the step-by-step processes of thought that we followed." Then with a bow he retired as an exuberant lady pushed him brusquely aside.

I do not know who this officer was, but I felt eternally grateful to him for the assurance he gave me. His words convinced me more strongly than ever that if on all occasions we use memory, reason and imagination in their proper and coherent order, we shall greatly increase our mental power and definitely clarify our thought.

Why has not so important a means of judgment been taught in our schools and colleges, you ask. Why have not all of us used it to strengthen our judgment? How is it possible that so simple a procedure has so escaped common use? The answer to this question is also quite as simple: which is—just because the process is so simple.

All the mighty aspects of life are simple. The deeper wisdoms escaped men for centuries, were unseen because they were so intimately present. Man's gaze was set on some complex ideal far ahead of him, while the wisdom he sought was before his face. This knowledge he ignored. It was too obvious for him to believe it contained great values.

It is from this over-reach of attention, this strain of purpose, that great truths have so often seemed illusive. They have evaded man's research for centuries simply because he made his effort far beyond where the knowledge lay. As we look back at the values our forefathers did not recognize, or the facts they did not see, do we not realize that they were ignored because they seemed so obvious? The would-be scholars could not believe them to be important. Apples had fallen to the ground for centuries, but it meant nothing to anyone until Sir Isaac Newton thought about it with special attention. Objects swung to and fro century after century; no idea of a pendulum came from it until Galileo watched a lantern swing in Pisa. Steam rose from a teakettle in many a kitchen without its power suggesting a steam engine to anyone.

All these common actions were too simple to seem significant. So has it always been. Man carried heavy loads for thousands of years, yet bits of log quite as round as wheels were about him everywhere. He had merely to see and think to discover the means upon which most transportation still depends.

Every bird's flight placed the secret of flying before everyone's eyes. By a warping of its wings a plane, which could not otherwise rise from the ground, took easily to the air.

When such discoveries appear in the field of modern mechanics, we nowadays become greatly excited about them, and avidly use the instruments that science presents to us. Research in the field of modern psychology has in recent years made a contribution to our health and happiness that should excite us far more than the invention of any of our modern machines. It has made the discovery of how a person uses his mind correctly, and thus how to live with ease. It has proved a fact of greater importance to each individual than all of our modern contrivances put together. Yet like the discovery of the wheel the needed truth was so simple that humans have ignored it for centuries. Especially was this basic wisdom hidden because it depended upon an attitude, and not until recent decades have the attitudes by which people live seemed important.

What is this grand yet simple discovery that can do so much for us? It consists in knowing how true mental power is made available to anyone who knows how to use it. It inheres in a proof that a man with great intelligence, who misuses his mind because he has the wrong attitude toward it, cannot think as well as a man with but a small part of such mental power who knows how to get his mind working for him.

In other words, modern psychology now offers you a way by which you can use your intelligence many, many times more successfully. By so doing you will not only conquer most of the troubles in your life, but achieve the desires that for years you have found impossible of realization.

The use of sensory equivalents, as thought patterns of your mind to follow, is the most important of such dynamic processes. To it we now add: *Don't identify yourself with your mind.*

You have doubtless at some time stood by a high-priced automobile, awed by its strength and marveling at its efficiency. You knew that it was a machine that could carry you with ease. You thought of the car as someone's possession.

A human mind is an even more wonderful instrument. It can work for one with ease. It *is* someone's possession. It is *not* the person himself. By means of the proper techniques it will respond automatically. This is a point of such significance that its importance cannot be exaggerated. Yet it is a point so simple that even now its greatness may elude you as it has eluded mankind for thousands of years.

Let us test out this matter in a personal way. Do you not

identify yourself as a person who thinks? Do you not make conscious effort to solve the problems that come to you? Did you not in school strive to do your lessons? Were you not told to discipline *yourself* in the doing of your tasks? Was not mental effort held up to you as a duty? Were you not trained to put all you had into your work, and to make yourself do it well?

Did you not, in other words, completely identify your mind with yourself as if you and your mind were one? How else did you think of yourself? How else could you think of yourself with the social and educational patterns coercing you to strive as a person to force yourself in your thinking? In any case, did anyone explain to you that your true effort should be put on the using of sensory equivalents of how you wished your mind as a possession of yours to work for you?

We know today that the old way of thinking is a slavery, exactly on a par with the way primitive man was bound to physical drudgery. We know that most everyone has been taught to be a mental serf, and that when set free of this horrible labor he finds himself suddenly—yes, that is the word: suddenly—free of the curse of debasing toil, and possessed of mental power of which he had not even dreamed.

So elusive, yet so simple, is this whole matter, we must here go very slowly in order not to have this point escape. Let us therefore retrace our steps a little. You have been taught to identify yourself with your mind. In doing this all the emotional confusions, personal tensions, egotistical attitudes, self-consciousness and psychoneurotic turmoils you may be burdened with become identified with your mind, and mental control is lost. Had you been taught that you are not your mind any more than you are your hands and feet, great would have been the difference in the way you used your intelligence. You would then have been able to give orders to your mind, functional patterns equivalent to your aims. You would not have needed to make troublesome effort. Does this fact seem so simple and obvious to you that it does not appear important? If so, you are making the same mistake that kept man for centuries from using wheels or knowing how to fly. It *is* a simple point, but one of utmost significance.

Your mind is like a great machine shop. It has a series of gifts and various possessions. *It is not yourself*. It is an organization of instruments that you can use *on demand* much as you use a motorcar, a typewriter, a sewing machine or a deep-freeze. Your mind will work for you if you tell it what you want it to do, and then let it do its task. It will work for you if you do not identify yourself with it. It will make effort for you if you do not yourself make effort save to create sensory equivalents for it to follow. If you keep relaxed and let your mind function for you, it will do for you what your motorcar does, which is to use its energy so that you need not use yours.

This is not an exaggerated statement. It is the result of a great discovery—one of the greatest of all discoveries—yet a fact so simple few people have seen it in many centuries. The early Egyptians, who built the pyramids, knew this truth. The Greek philosophers had glimmerings of it. Various geniuses have hinted at it, great men of science have used it, but without much awareness of what gave them their special power.

To the degree that you are concerned with your own mental brilliance you destroy a true relation to your mind, and can no longer treat it as a possession. To have pride of intellect or shame for your limitations puts your whole relation to true thinking out of order. To have your ego in any way concerned with the success of your thinking limits your power of thought, and destroys the purposive pattern that your mind requires. It does not then know what you want it to do.

If, on the other hand, you refuse to labor yourself, but let your mind do your thinking, it will work for you like a mighty genie. If you sit back, as it were, and do not push, but relax as you do when you let your car carry you, your mind will achieve for you a result as far beyond your past power as the capacity of your car is greater than your own two legs.

Learn therefore to "let go" and listen to the responses that your mind gives you. Let the parts of your great machine shop operate quietly. Your memory, when you do not crowd it by a state of panic, is a great instrument, one much more marvelous than mankind has ever invented. It will not work well when you push it beyond its own speed. To use it well you must obey it just as any good mechanic must obey the operational process of whatever machine he uses. Your reason is a magnificent device. It will solve problem after problem for you, if you use it in the way it was constructed to work. The clearer and more definite the sensory equivalents are of what you want your reason to do, the better it will function.

Your imagination is a mechanism so beyond the comprehension of most of us that we do not yet have a glimmer of the extent of its capacity and but dimly realize what it can do. You must let your imagination work for you in the way it was built to operate. You shut off its power when you yourself begin to pull levers and switches, and thus interfere with its smooth running. It will stand for no interference on the part of your ego. When dominated by you, it may stop entirely. You must *ask* your imagination to operate. You must let it know by means of a thought pattern what you desire of it in order for it to function to the full.

My only fear in writing this is that you will not believe how great a change can come into your life once you cease to identify yourself with your mind, but learn to use it as a series of great machines. I have a fear that you may do what mankind has done for so long a time, which is to think that this mighty point is so commonplace a procedure that it is not important and cannot accomplish what we believe it can.

Our whole educational system and the duty pattern of home and state are all against an acceptance of this greatest of all secrets. Let me beg you not to forget that the failure of humanity to think, feel and act in this way is why there are more people with mental breakdowns in our hospitals than from all other causes put together. If this is not a proof that we have been using our minds in the wrong way, then what is? Cause and effect are equal; there are no two ways around that fact.

You cannot keep happy and you cannot keep well in this great and speeded-up mechanical age unless you learn to stop your pick-and-shovel effort, and let the wonderful machines in your mind respond to your demands. They are your possessions. They are not yourself.

Learning to let your mind work for you, as you develop a sense of detachment, is the nineteenth concrete step in the art of living.

20 THE FUNCTIONAL PRINCIPLE

ITH all my heart and mind and strength I have tried to make clear to you the injury one causes the art of thinking when one identifies oneself with the processes of the mind. It is, however, a significant and, in a sense, a rather amusing fact that try as you will you cannot commit this crime in relation to most of the functions of your body. You do not operate any of the more important activities that go on inside of you. You cannot dominate them, and with many of them you cannot even interfere. You are forced to accept the fact of their automatic character.

If you would keep your psychic fingers from twiddling with your mind, and let it operate in its own way, as your body forces you to let it do, your life would become greatly eased.

The reason that nature made it impossible for you to interfere with many of the operative actions of your body is because you would soon kill yourself if you were allowed to become egotistical about the marvelous ways in which your organism works.

204

Many people, of course, injure their bodily activity. They do so by indulging in the wrong foods, drinks, late hours. In scores of other ways they delimit their physical efficiency. But these are not interferences caused by a willful wish to "run" the body. No one suddenly decides that he and his heart are one, and thus that it shall have no activity that he does not himself make an effort to accomplish. You do not *make* your blood circulate, or manage most of the amazing processes of your organism. They do not take place because you *strive* to have them happen. It would be a blessing to you beyond belief if you also gave up forcing the effort your mind delights in making.

That we may understand what is meant by the functional principles which act in mind and body, let us study some examples of it as science has revealed it at work within us.

Quite some years ago, Dr. Elié Metchnikoff, of the Pasteur Institute in France, discovered that when any injurious germs attack any part of the body, white blood corpuscles, like soldiers capturing a trench, rush at the enemy and flinging themselves at these intruders strive to overpower and consume them. This process is known by the solemn name of phagocytosis: the means by which microbes are destroyed. Modern surgery owes much of its efficiency to this discovery. The healing that results from the self-sacrifice of this army of white corpuscles is majestic and automatic. In all such organic procedures we have examples of a spontaneous response beyond any mechanical methods that mankind has ever conceived.

Most of such activities by which you live and continue to keep well are not self-created or self-directed. They function in yourself but they are not *of* yourself, as a willful personality. They take place in everyone else as well as in you, and to some degree in all that lives.

Obedient to its great designs, the cosmos moves and has its

being, fulfilling immutable laws. Its forces operate not only in the distant stars but also in you. What is the life process within you that automatically turns the juicy pulp of an apple or a lamb chop into the substances of your body? How does your organism know how to digest food and then to give it to your cells, so that, growing and multiplying, they build and rebuild your body, yes, and even your mind? It is not a process that you make come to pass any more than you decide to cause the next eclipse of the moon.

In his most fascinating book *This World of Ours*, written at the request of H. G. Wells, Dr. Abraham Glasser tells us that Dr. Oscar Schott, professor of anatomy and embryology at Amherst College, has striven to discover what this powerful automatism is and how it operates. After countless experiments he proved to his satisfaction that a certain stimulus invariably creates a certain response. This stimulator he called an "inductor." The late Dr. Hans Spemann, who was professor of biology at Freiburg University, received the Nobel prize, in 1935, for the results of similar research. He named this magical life force the "organizer." Each man worked in awe of the bionomic processes that they saw take place, always automatically and from no man's personal will.

In all such research the factor of plan, as the creative force of these principles, is made evident. No activity in the cosmos takes place until a design has been established. This is the predetermined templet that always organizes the resultant form. Nature and not a person himself makes these structures come into being and determines their use.

But here is a most significant point: that the dynamic functioning by which life operates is more than a matter of design if we think of design in a static sense. There is always a power that animates each design and thereby creates the forms of living substance. This is the instrumentality that makes a cell divide and in doing so continue its kind. The process goes on eternally in each species, a mysterious explosion by which the generative life of a variety is preserved. Nor is this all, for a still stranger influence sometimes appears, the evolutionary force that originates new species and their dynamic variations.

Nature is never static. The seed of a stone pine when it sprouts and grows produces a tree that, while still a pine, is just as different from a red or a white pine as is such a conifer from any other tree. From the acorn of a live oak the sturdy black oak of New England will never come. Nor will the live oak survive the northern blasts. Cut the leaves of either tree and the new ones that appear will always be those of that special variety.

So also with the cells of all animals and clearly so with man. But what, may we ask, is this mysterious power that directs the functional process by which cells create specificity of tissue? How is it that a transformation of cells takes place so that the parts of the human body develop? What is the power that gives us a heart, lungs, ears and a mouth? What bionomic design controls (as the Mendelian theory demonstrates) even the color of a person's eyes?

Let us go further into this mystery. A lobster is not a creature high in the evolutionary scale, yet if it loses one of its claws the cells in its body know how to grow a new one. Nor does the lobster have to boss the job. It happens. In your organism, if you are injured or operated upon, the same magic force that originated each part of your body sends the cells rushing to heal whatever wound you receive. After a time your organism is made well again, but you do not make it so.

Is it not possible that this amazing automatism will also work in your mind? Is it not possible that a cosmic energy is the cause of it all and that your life could be repaired without your effort if you would let it come to pass? May it not be that it is the interferences of egotism and of social ignorance that have denied you the spontaneous creative guidance that was yours as an embryo and to a great extent even as a child? Can it not be that your mind possesses the same dynamic processes that function so majestically on the physical plane?

The human body gives us magnificent examples of automatism. When any part of the organism is injured all the rest of this amazing structure goes at once to work, concentrating on a repair of the injury. Protections form around a blood vessel or an injured muscle. Where cartilage is needed it is made out of transformed muscle fiber. Blood clots develop to retard undue pressures and assist in the healing. Remove one kidney and its partner becomes twice as large, capable of doing the other's work. Cut an artery and the blood vessels contract. The volume of blood in the body then automatically increases to compensate for what was lost. Balance is soon restored so that the circulation can continue at its normal rate. When a wound festers it is because, as we have already said, the white corpuscles have gathered to help contest the bacteria. The pus is a wall of their dead bodies erected against the bacterial attack. All this happens inside of you without the least conscious effort on your part, an example of the way your mental and spiritual life could also take place.

After patient research into such mysteries as these, Dr. Gustave Levander, chief surgeon in one of the great hospitals in Sweden, was able to prove that an etheric fluid exists apart from the cells. He filtered this almost invisible substance so that no cells existed in the solution. Later, when he injected the liquid into living muscle, he found that the original struc ture from which the fluid came began to grow. Centuries before, Swedenborg, another Swedish genius and the greatest anatomist of his time, named a similar substance "the lymbus," and spoke again and again of an invisible and etheric fluid that animated the body and gave directive energy to the cells.

In any case, there seems now to be no question that the "organizer" that Dr. Spemann studied, the "inductor," Schott called it, is the "master builder" of Dr. Levander's research and quite possibly the invisible life fluid, or lymbus, concerning which Swedenborg was so impressed.

The point which is important to us in our research as to getting rid of strain is that there is no logical reason to suppose that this dynamic automatic process stops with the body. Such a conclusion is in fact illogical, since we are in every sense integrated organisms. We know that whatever affects the body creates effects in the mind, and whatever affects the mind also causes effects in the body. This is a fact too well established to argue.

There is then a substance within you that automatically sets itself in motion and if allowed to function will operate on and within your organism. By various means its activity can be inhibited, repressed, congested, suppressed and stopped. Tourniquets restrict it, toxics poison it, tensions limit it, certain drugs counteract its activity. But the fact that it is there no one can deny.

Is it not also apparent that this vital energy acts on the mind as well and is psychical as well as physical? Swedenborg so stated, and many students of psychosomatic medicine believe this to be true.

That being the case, is it not also logical that negative mental attitudes, constrictive states of mind, fear patterns, tension-producing thoughts and emotions can also inhibit, repress, congest, suppress and stop the mental activity of this "master builder," this psychosomatic "inductor"? And have we not here the cause of failure, misfortune and psychoneurosis? Can we hope, if we allow destructive beliefs to constrict the activity of this "organizer," to have anything but failure result?

Let us reason a step further. Have we not also here, when constructively used and understood, a formative producer of success, health and happiness? If constrictive mental states and negatively set emotions can inhibit and so congest the activity of this life-giving substance as to produce disease, cannot constructive attitudes and positively conditioned emotions open up the flow and allow these automatic dynamics to carry on their mysterious and magical purposes so as to produce health and happiness? No other conclusion is logical.

We thus can affirm at long last that we are approaching knowledge that proves beyond dispute that living easily is possible, a fact that heretofore was an intuitive optimism. To know that this resurgent vigor is real, and not a hopeful hypothesis, is an encouragement beyond our fondest anticipation.

To remain so receptive and so relaxed in all that you do that a dynamic energy motivates your every act is the twentieth concrete step in the joyous experience of living.

21 INSTRUMENTATION

THE realization that your mind is a powerful organism which works for you, if you let it do so, is the most practical of all issues concerning the activity of human nature. It also permits one to develop a most useful attitude known as *instrumentation*. This point of view has been ignored by sophisticated people because it has been thought to be a philosophical and religious concept. It has also been given an ethical value. It is far more important than that. We are here concerned with the simple truth that to treat oneself as an instrument, rather than as an ego, is an essential procedure if one is to gain the best results from his mental endowment. Not otherwise can one achieve without strain.

As an actual fact, egotism of position and pride of accomplishment are in every sense ridiculous. None of us asked to be born. We did not create our natures. To have brains is not a credit to us. To lack them is no fault of ours. We inherit our mental equipment. Our responsibility is to use it; our sole credit is how we do so.

The attitude that the mind is a unit of great machinery is a first and major step to the further recognition that we as selves are also organisms capable of doing what we can in a given situation. It permits us to use and to depend upon sensory equivalents of efficient conduct that releases our mental powers to their full. It removes strain from life, and nervous concern about the outcome of effort.

Some understanding of this impersonality, and of its value in self-expression, has been at times possessed by the great accomplishers. Novalis worded it well when he wrote: "The artist belongs to his work, not the work to the artist." Michelangelo expressed an equivalent concept. "Art," he wrote, "is a jealous thing; it requires the whole and entire man." To James Russell Lowell we must give credit for the best definition of all: "Genius is that in whose power a man is." Prior tinged his statement with the moral value that has so often made instrumentation repulsive to sturdy personalities: "Thy sum of duty let two words contain: be humble and be just."

None of these men seems to have grasped the release of power or the new freedom that comes from this way of viewing the self. They did not see that it allows us to ignore much of what we would as egos have been impelled to do, or realize how much more easily it permits a task to be done. Fenelon expressed the former, and Victor Hugo the latter, of these great privileges. "Be content," wrote Fenelon, "with doing calmly the little which depends upon yourself, and let all else be to you as if it were not." Hugo declared: "Art needs no spur beyond itself," by which he meant that it contains its own impelling. "Ideas often flash across our minds more completely than we could make them," La Rochefoucauld explained, because, of course, of the receptive power that instrumentation endows.

Of them all, only Douglas Jerrold saw that we have a right

to give up those social obligations that, when egotism is no longer involved, are not felt by us as natural impellings. "Man owes two solemn debts," he wrote, "one to society and one to nature. It is only when he pays the second that he covers the first."

We might deepen this profound insight by quoting from Schiller: "Art is the right hand of nature; the latter has only given us being, the former has made us men." And, "A man, be the heavens ever praised, is sufficient for himself," said Carlyle.

The attitude of instrumentation then takes nothing from you as a personality. It is not a doctrine of abnegation or a creed of denial. You do not discard yourself. You greatly revere yourself as an instrument of use. This attitude of using the self has in it, when well understood, a subtle paradox: that by surrendering a right to power more power is given. This fact is as true as that mighty saying: "He that loseth his life . . . shall find it."

Every great man of science knows the truth of this attitude, for he it is who so dedicates himself to the finding of truth that pride of achievement ceases to be. "Let us have faith that right makes might," Lincoln said, "and in that faith let us to the end dare to do our duty *as we* understand it." That word "as" is as great here as it is in the second of the commandments given by the Master of Galilee: "Thou shalt love thy neighbour *as thyself.*"

There is no loss of self-respect, no abnegation and no self-denial if one ponders deeply that little word "as." There is not only a true self-regarding, but a reverence for all the great powers given to the self as well as to all humanity.

Let us realize then that the attitude of instrumentation is not a sniveling degradation, nor an abject surrender of one's rights as a man. It is a way of life by which power is gained rather than lost. Its contradictions are apparent rather than real, even as in what Achilles Poincelot wrote of art: "There are certain epochs in art when simplicity is audacious originality."

There is in the attitude of instrumentation the same simplicity of being which leads also to audacious originality. It also gives the only lasting joy. "When a man has put his heart into his work and done his best, he feels relieved and gay, but what he had done or said otherwise shall give him no peace," wrote Emerson. To this we might add, from Washington Irving: "The only happy author in this world is he who is below care of reputation." Edmund Burke saw clearly that there was no loss of personal strength in this attitude toward how one's mind was used. He believed one should reverence the "strength and dignity of mind, and vigor and activity of body, which enable men to conceive and execute great actions."

All about us nature manifests the principle of instrumentation. Each flower, each tree and every animal grows as it can and does what it can. Their responsibility begins and ends with the use of the attributes given to them to the end of fulfilling their inherent possibilities.

Put into one paragraph, we might define this impersonality as a realization that we ourselves are not only instruments but combinations of instruments, most of which are capable of functioning automatically if allowed to do so. The attitude of instrumentation permits them so to act. It also endows a new and deeper sense of identity, an awareness of self not only above and beyond our bodies but above and beyond our minds. It allows our minds freedom to do their work.

Of all the slaveries in the world, that of pride of accomplishment is the most imprisoning, for there is then no freedom from the consequences of one's actions. The egotist is bound to his duty as a dictator to his despotism. There is then no escape from the durance of constant toil. He must justify himself or die. Victim of his self-evaluation, the treadmill of arrogance stretches long years ahead with no end save that of the ultimate desolation of his own society.

It is strange that anyone would select such a fate, and yet it is the choice of millions. Under its duress they bear endless strain, becoming tense and nervous when their position is threatened, doomed to the exhaustions of unhealthful sleep.

In contrast to this, a joyous freedom is made possible by the attitude of creative impersonalism: by the realization that all nature asks of us is for us to make the rather slight effort to create sensory equivalents as functional patterns of our purposes. We thereby use our powers as best we can, when and as we can, with no concern for the results of our effort. We are thus free of the greatest cause of unhappiness: the coercions of obligation.

You and I have certain abilities and certain lacks in the machine shops of our minds. I would make the poorest public accountant that ever attempted to use figures. You might not be as at ease as I am on a lecture platform. John Doeman is perhaps mechanical but color blind. His wife is artistic but finds it difficult even to use a can opener. The can seems persistently to buckle. Would it not be foolish for John to spend his life trying to paint landscapes, or his wife to become an expert mechanic?

Behind this contrast of endowments is a principle which pertains to far more than mechanical and artistic proclivities. It is concerned with the facts of identity. You and I are not just persons. We are a kind of person, suited as are plants and animals to certain uses and not easily adapted to others. In short, we are just as much instruments of varying types as are motorcars, kitchen stoves, beds and tables. No stove is an efficient means of transportation, nor is cooking easily carried out by using an automobile, no matter how hot the engine becomes. Tables are hard to sleep upon, and beds, while usable for a breakfast snack, would not well accommodate a four-course dinner. Each of these structures is an instrument. You do not ask it to do what it was not constructed to do. You expect it to perform the service for which it was made.

The same principle holds, or should hold, for human nature. I knew an elderly farmer down in Maine who, when asked to perform some task for which he did not feel endowed, always said, "I wun't, I don' hefter." From him I learned to say, "I won't, I don't have to." Such a statement is not an anarchism, for in it there is no neglect of the act of doing the duties that one's mind and body can fulfill. They are not accomplished as duties, however, but as uses of one's inherent endowments.

One of the tenets of the new psychology is expressed in the phrase: If you find and use the best course of action, the best results will come to pass of their own accord. Keep your attention on the control and use of good causes of thought and behavior. Never concern yourself with the outcomes. In other words, use your wits as best you can. Make sensory equivalents of the way you desire to have them work, and the results will then be the best that your mind can at the time produce. While doing this, give up mechanical idealism, that desperate, idiotic perfectionism which kills millions yearly.

You are not God, and it does no good to try to usurp His power or position. Ideals were never meant to be fulfilled. It is, in fact, utterly impossible to fulfill them, for the better your abilities are able to do, the higher your ideals will be, and always out of reach. Straining to achieve them only accomplishes stress, and a kind of closing down or stoppage of your mental machinery. Your nerves then become tense, your glands disfunction, your viscera get out of order. Your body no longer sustains your mind. How then can it do its work efficiently? Having already interfered with its automatic action from the attitude of personalism, is not more failure inevitable?

Instrumentation cannot be achieved until one gives up egotism and does so utterly. He who loses his ego finds his power. This is a true paraphrase of the ancient teaching. A simple attitude of usefulness is essential to poise and peace. From its blessing comes an abandonment of all predatory competition. The freed soul competes with himself, but with no one else. He does not need the spur of comparison. Dedicated to the belief that he has a certain usefulness to perform, he is glad of the excitement of conquest. It is victory in his task, not victory over anyone who is also striving, that is his concern.

The great blessing that comes from instrumentation is the abolishment of the old coercive and oppressive duties which caused such killing pressure. One suddenly discovers he has only one duty to perform, that of being himself. He thus uses his mind as fully, as truly and as easily as is possible at any given moment. The measure of his power is not static. He may possess more wisdom and more dynamic tomorrow, but that is not his concern. All he is asked to do, and all he asks himself to do, is to let his mind fulfill its possibilities of today. That is enough, and it is a great deal.

He who is grateful for his quantum of imagination, of reason, of judgment, of memory, and uses his five senses as the basis of a sturdy common sense need not worry as to his accomplishments. They will take place of their own accord, fulfilling the sensory equivalents his desire has created.

There is no glory like this freedom, no way of life so blessed as that of instrumentation, no success so sure as that of those who have gotten egotism out of the way. They it is in whom sensory equivalents develop spontaneously.

For the sake of emphasis, let me repeat that from the attitude of instrumentation one views oneself as an organism and all one's attributes as gifts. He thinks of them as possessions just as the clothes he has are his but not himself. It is a frame of mind built on a recognition that none of us created the abilities with which we have been biologically endowed.

This attitude is based on a recognition that we have many of our attributes in common, such as sight, hearing, touch, our mental processes, imagination, reason, memory and the various functions of our make-up, such as tenderness, a sense of nurture, a love of kindness that makes one human.

There is also a realization that our special abilities are given to us by our blood stream, and that it is not only foolish to have pride concerning them but stupid also. As well as having souls we possess mental machinery that will work for us as dynamic instruments when we embody our desire in sensory equivalents and then let them function for us.

This great creative process sets the mind free to function according to its kind. One's whole effort is in the making of sensory equivalents of his wants for the mind to follow. One does not have to *make* it function. Its impulse to act constructively is as natural as the gift of a seagull to fly. Faith that the mind, if allowed to do its work, *will* do it spontaneously and automatically is the secret that removes the constriction from its dynamic energy.

All animals except man know how to behave and to make full use of their abilities. Mankind would know but for the interference of self-consciousness and social (familial) suppression, which always delimits the power to create sensory equivalents of one's desires. There is no stupidity greater than personalized pride, and none that causes more misfortune.

From earliest childhood ninety-nine out of every hundred individuals are forced into egotistical attitudes by the ignorant manhandling of their natures on the part of the adults in their lives. Home training, education and some so-called moral and religious influences are truly on an untrue basis. Since no child made his own nature it is unjust and irreligious to treat him as if he had. Seeing this truth, the ancient Romans coined the word *proprium*, meaning that we are taught to appropriate to ourselves in a prideful and possessive way all that has been given to us by nature.

Those who learn to make sensory equivalents as purposive patterns for their minds to follow, and who respect and have gratitude that their mental capacities can respond to this thought design, are the ones who develop a creative impersonality. These are they who let their endowments work for them. There is no attitude that so completely takes pressure out of life as that of instrumentation. And none so endows that pregnant intuition that is the soul of genius. It is also the secret of the deeper understandings in anyone's being.

Instrumentation also frees one utterly from the stress of human relations. You will find that if people easily get into conflict with each other, it is the ego in one or both of them that causes the antagonism.

Consider the case of L.P.M. His relation to other people has been in confusion all his life. He is always anxious as to his position in the world, over-anxious as to his rights. A power drive impels him to enforce others to recognize his importance. He is constantly explaining what he has done. People, of course, are offended by the perpetual effrontery of his personality. Yet he does not realize that this is why they refuse him the necessary co-operation. The world is all wrong and people selfish and stupid in the opinion of L.P.M. Had the spirit of instrumentation been in control of his way of life, no such stress would have tortured his days.

Consider, in contrast, the experience of Nathan Ellison. He

is an inventor, who now manufactures the machine he has conceived. He does not feel proud of his accomplishment, nor even that his invention is entirely his creation. He believes that new ideas originate in one's mind from many sources —what other people say and do, what one observes, and sometimes from intuition. But is not any intuition a form of guidance beyond the self? he asks.

As a result of his attitude, his employees and all his friends love him, and gladly do all they can to increase his success.

The more you allow your ego to dominate you, the more trouble you will have in life. This assertive thrust for one's supposed rights is the greatest cause of marital discord, and the primary producer of divorce. Do not, however, suppose for a moment that egotism is the only means of self-protection. He who believes in instrumentation develops a passionate conviction that he has a right to guard the body, mind and soul that nature has given to him. When he believes that a certain course of action is true, and the one that he should follow, no persuasion or coercion can stop him or dissuade him from his chosen way. An egotist is not half as stubborn.

You have only to study the biographies of some of the great men and women of the past to observe the dynamic energy they exerted in defense of their beliefs and their right to protect themselves as instruments of creative accomplishment and human service. Not all the conservative prejudices of all England could have stopped Florence Nightingale from fulfilling her destiny.

Maintaining a spirit of gratitude for all the endowments that life gave you, and using them as you would any other possession or gift, is the twenty-first step in the forming of one single and simple process that when learned releases one from tension forever.

22 THE USE OF INSPIRATION

*J*UST to the degree that one has become "converted" from a worship of his own ego, and has accepted instrumentation as a way of life, is intuition a true and dynamic possession. Just to the degree that a man thinks, feels and acts as an agent of accomplishment will any form of inspiration become a useful power. To whatever measure his work is compromised by personalism the gift of intuition is shut off.

Self-aggrandizement turns any and all guidance into nonsense. Predatory competition and the debasement of others deflates, and deflates utterly, the latent genius in a man from which creative energy could otherwise flow.

Much has been written against intuition by critically minded intellectualists. They have derided it as an unsound process. They have done so with good reason: it *is* unsound for *them*. It is untrustworthy for all who do not understand what intuition is and hence have no faith in it. It is an unsafe guidance for an egotist.

At the same time these arrogant slaves of effort, while they produce driblets of conscious thought, make a great to-do in their desire to deny the statements and effective results of the great accomplishers. They insist that any way of thinking other than their own cannot be right. It pains them that the leaders of men will not come down to their pedestrian basis and get off the high horse of inspiration.

No great thinker denies the values of logic or the usefulness of the various forms of reason. He knows that one needs them to form sure judgments. But a genius will not exalt the body of logic above the insight that gives it soul.

Patient calculation is a form of labor. It must be done when no other means is available, just as you must use your hands and feet for those tasks that cannot or have not yet been accomplished by swifter and surer means. We need not abandon the intellect even if without intelligence it is relatively valueless, nor yet forsake intelligence because the intellect can so skillfully dress it up. Either-or thinking, caused by a subservient surrender of thought to the all-or-none activities of the nerves, has been the curse of curses in man's attempt to understand himself and his relation to life.

There is no either-or choice sanely possible in this matter of logical reason versus spontaneous intuition. In this life both are needed, even as a man requires a body for his soul and a soul for his body.

There has been much written in recent years as to the nature of the human mind. It is now—in the opinion of the more intelligent psychologists—divided into the conscious, the coconscious and the unconscious levels. The coconscious is that region between awareness and what has been called the subliminal depths, the area where ideas are half remembered and thoughts are on the "tip of the tongue" but cannot quite be said. That which remains unconscious belongs to the under-current of thought and emotion.

These rather obvious divisions of the mind are not adequate, however. We cannot relegate all that is not conscious to an undifferentiated unconscious level. There are wide contrasts between the subliminal hates, fears and virulent rages of the nether depths and the ineffable qualities of love, faith and courage which rise spontaneously from within our natures.

This being so, a second great division becomes essential: a separation of the unconscious level into the subconscious and the supraconscious (sometimes called the superconscious). Had man not possessed a supraconscious level of being, no majestic music, no consummate art, no great inventions, no inspiration and prophetic insight could have taken place.

It is by the activity of the supraconscious that intuition is made possible. All the power of religion, philosophy, ethics and the prophetic and creative aspects of life depend essentially on intuition. Without it they would have no soul and could not be. To its active presence we owe what we call genius.

I have at other times and in other books written of the *esse*, or constructive sense of identity in the supraconscious, as a higher form of what Freud called the Id, or barbaric awareness in the subconscious. The *esse* is that attribute of the mind that is alert to the reception of inspiration and sensitive to intuitive mentation. In the same contexts I have made note of the constructive flow of the designing or architectural force that rises from this center of being, making clear that a receiving power merges with the designing action of growth and ex-pression. The creative forces are dynamic aspects of the *esse* as the identity center of the supraconscious.

We need not here go into the seemingly mysterious powers of this union of creative attributes producing what is called the *telarche*. We are concerned at this point with application rather than with theory. Let us, nevertheless, realize that there are concrete and provable attributes of personality capable of engendering intuition. That being so, we can concern ourselves with its practical use. By a faith in the power and accuracy of intuition, it will then function for us, reducing effort and strikingly improving results.

Through the years, various writers have mentioned men and women who lived from such a divine afflatus, experiencing a subliminal uprush of intuition and energy. More recently, Dr. Pitirim A. Sorokin, of Harvard, has made a survey of those who were impelled by such a dynamic urge. His study of the ease with which one can use intuition is of major importance. A list of those who have done so appears in his excellent book, *The Ways and Power of Love*. He gives in this treatise what reviewers call a "scientific evidence of the existence in man of a supreme, creative power" from which intuition springs.

A person may know all the rules of art, music or literature, he tells us, yet if he fails to listen to and use the intuitional flow that the supraconscious makes possible, he is only a "remote relative of the Shakespeares and Chaucers, the Bachs and Beethovens."

It should not be supposed, however, that intuition makes reason unnecessary. No such ridiculous swing to extremes is ever contemplated by a thoughtful and well-balanced person. Rather is intuition used to empower reason, not to abolish it. The two work together as one, in a well-disciplined mind.

There are, moreover, many techniques that require a creative union of these two great attributes of judgment. We have space here to touch upon only a few of them.

Someone stole a large ham from an Indian while he was away from his hut. He returned from his hunting trip so soon after the intruder had left that mud from the man's boots was still wet on his rough floor. He gave one swift look around, then rushed to find the sheriff in the nearby village. A short, white man, lame in the left leg and with only two fingers on his right hand, had stolen the ham, he said, and at three o'clock in the afternoon. The intruder had gone north on foot and could be caught about four miles beyond the village.

Knowing how astute a thinker the old Indian was, the sheriff jumped into his car and in short order had the thief arrested, the ham still clutched in his hand. How did the Indian know the facts that he presented to the man of the law? Intuition played a part, there can be no doubt about that, but it was merged with good observation and a keen power of reasoning.

All the Indians in the region wore moccasins. The thief, as the mud and his footprints proclaimed, wore boots. The fellow was short, because he could not reach the high-hanging ham without standing on a chair. He had stood with his back to the window, for he could not otherwise have seen how to untie the ham with the sun in his eyes. So it would have been at three o'clock. He had also used his left hand to hold the knife, for a scratch on the wall when the knife had slipped could not otherwise have been made from where the man stood on the chair.

The ham had been wrapped in paper. This he had torn in taking it down. A piece lay on the floor with a clear imprint of a two-fingered hand, the stumps showing where the fingers had been lost. Lastly, the footprints, which pointed north, had an unevenness that only a lame man could produce. The marks revealed that the left leg dragged. Nor could he have gone far with such a handicap.

No intelligent thinker would wish to abandon keen observation or careful reasoning for even the best of intuition. Yet is it not clear that the swiftness of the old Indian's judgment had a something more to it than visual calculation? What he saw and reasoned became unified by his power of intuition.

In the process of analysis, by which the old Indian recognized what the thief was like, he did not restrict any aspect of thought that came into his mind. By what we call the flotation process, which is the art of thinking by the juxtaposition of contrasts and opposites, incorrect conclusions were discarded until the true facts appeared. Gold is now salvaged by this method in the smelting industry. Since oil and water will not mix, the oil when rising to the surface brings the gold flakes with it. One's thought, to succeed with this method of comparison, however, must be free floating and full.

One of the serious mistakes of the average person is that instead of believing in and using the philosophy of plenty, and thus flooding into his desire as nature does into hers, he focuses his mind on some one petty aspect of his purpose and becomes morose because that special aspect is not at once solved to his liking.

"But that's about the way everyone does," he will tell you, as if following the example of the mob was intelligent. The hodgepodge we miscall civilization is riddled with the consequences of an economics of scarcity in great contrast to nature's lavish way. No life policy could be more unwise.

When man ignores the methods by which nature succeeds, he usually fails. Sometimes he has "luck" for a while, for every rule has its exception. Such deviations from the norm do not prove anything except that they are deviations. Like the breaking of the bank at Monte Carlo, the luck works once. If tried persistently it leads to destitution.

One of the most obvious of nature's methods, and one that millions ignore, is this flooding technique. How many seeds do you suppose an ordinary plant produces in contrast to the number that find a place in the soil, take root and grow? How many little trees developed for a while, then died, before a grove of giants towered into the sky? How many drops of rain find their way into sap, or into some other useful aspect of growth in comparison to those that rush down a river bed to the sea? How many herring in the ocean live to become mature fish, able to produce their young? If there were not millions more than those who survive the preying upon them of hungry salmon and swooping gulls, how long would the herring species continue? Nature on every hand uses the flooding technique, and by this means carries out her will.

Before I secured the home of my dreams, which I described in the chapter on Repetitive Strategy, I had written one hundred and sixty-four letters to all sorts of people in the general region I had finally decided was the part of America where I would be likely to find more of my wishes fulfilled. I read the friendly answers to these letters in a sort of drowsy state, such as one experiences under the power of inspiration. This is the mood in which intuition best works. Then I marked on a map the spot where I felt my home would be. It proved out as the exact spot where I found it. It was the first place I went to when my trip to the region began. No time was wasted, for intuition, merged with reason and based on the flooding process, had done its work.

We need, however, a still more important thinking method that will help us find the truth in what people say and write to us. We need to be able to sift the facts out of the suppositions.

That great philosopher, Socrates, depended largely on intuition merged with reason as a means of founding his basis of thought. He spoke of himself as a "midwife"—one who helped intelligent ideas to be born.

Some decades ago, Sir Patrick Geddes said that everyone ought to read Plato at least once a year, in order to study the Socratic method so well reported on by that eminent thinker. Sir Patrick had in mind that most people become confused as to what the real values are in any situation, and fail to see what opinions are true and what are false.

You will recall that Sir Patrick was knighted because he became the greatest historian and sociologist of his time, treating each of these subjects as functionally as a biologist would deal with the growing and changing process of the living organism. In other words, he was skillful in the art of seeing the causes of the conditions that developed in the body politic within and between nations. He was also the most intuitive man I have ever known, and the most ardent believer in this majestic power. But he never allowed it to occlude his power of reason.

"People," Sir Patrick told me, "need to study the history of their own lives so as to discover what caused their troubles, what those difficulties are and how long they will last."

"You mean," I asked, "that by knowing and using what is called the Socratic method one can more easily discover what the real situation is in each case?"

"Exactly that," he asserted with his characteristic intensity. "Millions waste their lives, and become worn out, because they don't know how to separate a real cause from an obscuring effect. Anyone can become exhausted trying to correct effects. You wouldn't spank a baby because, having the measles, it became irritable, would you?" His Scotch eyes peered out at me from under his bushy brows.

"Certainly not," I hastened to agree.

"Well, people do that all the time in response to the behavior of others, and so make a hubbub out of life."

Sir Patrick loved to use babies, and how one would treat them, as examples of human conduct. I once heard him give a lecture on *The City Beautiful*, using one's attitude toward a baby as the central theme.

In dealing with our own problems, we might do well to use

illustrations that have the same simplicity as has the behavior of babies to help us to see the pressure people put upon us, thus confusing us by erudite intellectualism and obscuring intelligent understanding. We also might do well to analyze all situations as Socrates would have done, reaching below the surface appearances to find the true motivations.

This method, as now used, is termed the *gimlet*, because it bores through the external levels to find the hidden aspect of a situation.

The method consists in asking a question, then questioning the answer to that question; next questioning the second answer, then questioning the third answer; and so on and on down to the primary cause. Nothing but the questioning of answers is used. By this means, Socrates exposed and exploded the illogical ideas of his students and helped them to discover the reality of facts. By this method you can discover the truth or falsity of whatever information is put before you.

One would like to give many more of such dynamic methods, not only because of their usefulness, but to prove that reason is not abandoned but empowered when intuition merges with it. The process is, we know, inherent and natural in the mental procedures of genius. More than this, it is the means by which it unifies conscious and unconscious mentation. Years ago, Myers wrote: "Genius should rather be regarded as a power of utilising a wider range than other men can utilise, of faculties in some degree innate in all: a power of appropriating the results of subliminal mentation to subserve the supraliminal stream of thought, so that an 'inspiration of genius' will be in truth a subliminal uprush, an emergence into the current of ideas which the man is consciously manipulating, of other ideas which he has not consciously originated, but which have shaped themselves beyond his will, in profounder regions of his being."

Research proves to us that many a child has gifts not unlike those of genius, but that education and social pressure often press them into the depths of consciousness so that contact with the power is lost.

Archbishop Watley possessed an amazing mathematical gift in childhood but lost it after he went to school. He writes of it as follows: "There was certainly something peculiar in my calculating faculty. It began to show itself at between five and six, and lasted about three years. I soon got to do the most difficult sums, always in my head, for I knew nothing of figures beyond numeration. I did these sums much quicker than anyone could upon paper, and I never remember committing the smallest error. When I went to school, at which time the passion wore off, I was a perfect dunce at ciphering and have continued so ever since."

Still more remarkable, perhaps, was Professor Safford's loss of power. Safford's whole bent was mathematical; his boyish gift of calculation raised him into notice. He became a professor of astronomy and "had therefore every motive and every need to retain the gift, if thought and practice could have done so. But whereas at ten years of age he worked correctly in his head, in one minute, a multiplication sum the answer to which consisted of thirty-six figures, he is, I believe, neither more nor less capable of such calculation than his neighbors."

We have a similar case in a Mr. Van R., of Utica. Myers states that he "at the age of six years distinguished himself by a singular faculty for calculating in his head. At eight he entirely lost this faculty, and after that time he could calculate neither better nor faster than any other person. He did not retain the slightest idea of the manner in which he performed his calculations in childhood."

By way of contrast, Myers also tells us that, with a man named Bidder, the gift persisted throughout life. "His paper, in

Volume XV, of the Proceedings of the Institute of Civil Engineers, while furnishing a number of practical hints to the calculator, indicates also a singular readiness of communication between different mental strata. Whenever, he says (page 255) I feel called upon to make use of the stores of my mind, they seem to rise with the rapidity of lightning. And in Volume CIII, of the same proceedings, Mr. W. Pole, F. R. S., in describing how Mr. Bidder could determine mentally the logarithm of any number to seven or eight places, says, 'He had an almost miraculous power of seeing, as it were, intuitively what factors would divide any large number, not a prime. Thus, if he were given the number 17,861, he would instantly remark it was three hundred and thirty-seven times fifty-three. . . . He could not, he said, explain how he did it, it seemed as natural as instinct.' "

In this reference, Myers states: "Childhood is genius without capacity. It makes for most of us our best memory of inspiration, and our truest outlook upon the real, which is the ideal, world. From a great distance we can watch the inward stir of mighty thought, the same for Aeschylus, for Newton, for Vergil: A stir independent of worldly agitation, like the swing and vibration of the tide-wave across the ocean, which takes no note of billow or of storm.

"Nay, we can see against the sun, 'The eagle soaring above the tomb of Plato,' and in Paul, as in Plotinus, we can catch that sense of self-fulfillment, of rapture, of deliverance, which the highest minds have bequeathed to us as the heritage of their highest hours. These, our spiritual ancestors, are no eccentrics, nor degenerates: They have made for us the sanest and most fruitful experiment yet made by man: they have endeavored to exalt the human race in a way in which it can in truth be exalted: they have drawn on forces which exist, and on a soul which answers: they have dwelt on those things

231

'by dwelling on which it is,' as Plato has it, 'That even God is divine.' "

You may be one who heretofore has been skeptical of the accuracy of intuition, and doubtful that inspiration really exists. You may also be a believer in both of these somewhat esoteric abilities, but unable heretofore to use them yourself. As a child you undoubtedly depended in some measure upon intuition as well as inspiration, but you did not know how to protect them against the challenges and skepticism of the adults about you. Thus, while you did not lose these gifts, you more or less lost contact with them, coming to depend upon the factual reasoning that your superiors forced upon you.

If this is the case, the first step is to believe that you once upon a time were intuitive and did have inspirational power. Follow this by experimenting, even as men of science do in a laboratory, to see how often you can make intuition work, and at what times and in what ways inspiration will serve you. Pay attention to your hunches. If you still doubt that it is safe to carry them out, as guidance, do not do so. But observe afterward whether or not they were true directions.

If you find that your hunches were often right, you will soon have more faith in intuition and inspirational power. This trust will make you use these guides more often and soon you will have creative perception at your command.

Learning to live by drawing from forces that exist in the cosmos, yet that are closely around us, is the twenty-second concrete step in the one great art of living dynamically.

23 A CENTER OF POWER

*M*ODERN science has recently taught us that the universe is an essential element of a cosmic unity of which man is an integral part. We now know that we live in an electromagnetic creation that must be maintained in complete balance. What affects one part of this inherent whole affects every other.

Even a century ago such a statement would have belonged only to the abstruse theories of the philosophers. Today it is important to the man in the street and is bringing to pass the new practicality which is upon us. Only by knowing this basic adjustment and using it can one hope to survive and to maintain poise in an era so intensified and speeded up as ours.

This concept of a new practicality means that we must, at long last, make use of the fact that all laws, methods and means that belong to the world of substance are now reduced by science to densities, intensities and frequencies of vibration, which pertain also to us. We must apply the fact that every

233

process that belongs to the subjective manifestation of nature concerns the procedures of personality. Not an action, not a principle of chemistry or physics, of mechanics or agriculture, exists that does not also include the human personality.

We were once told by eminent philosophers that man is an epitome of the universe. It sounded like a nice, pretty speculation. We know today that it is a fact so true we cannot organize our lives and neglect it. We also realize that those great accomplishers we have called geniuses were not so different from other people. Each and all possessed, however, one distinguishing power: they felt not only that they were in the universe, but that the universe was in them. They intuitively knew that its dynamic flow was their impelling. The cosmic powers were *their* powers.

Since some of them were not religious in any ecclesiastical sense, we cannot agree with what Haydon believed when he wrote: "The greatest geniuses have always attributed everything to God, as if conscious of being possessed of a spark of His divinity," for there were atheists among the towering minds. As for myself, I can testify to the truth of Haydon's idea only to the degree that a divine spark and reception of divine guidance are to me the very basis of ease in living. On the other hand, the great Thomas Huxley was not only an agnostic but it was he who coined the term.

Much has been said and written concerning a divine influx of wisdom and power. Our libraries are full of tomes describing the mystical energies of the soul. There is, however, an almost utter absence of information as to how one may contact and release this dynamic strength.

As practical men we shall not go far if we push this power away from us by considering it to be a strange, occult capacity. Thus with another of Haydon's ideas we can emphatically agree. He wrote that "genius is nothing more than our common faculties refined to a greater intensity. There are no astonishing ways of doing astonishing things."

At the same time, there is nothing commonplace about this center of guidance within us. "All the means of action," Longfellow told us, "the shapeless mass, the materials are about us. What we need is the celestial fire to change the flint into transparent crystal."

We more easily contact this celestial fire if we realize that it was once an energy that impelled us and gave us strength. Scientific research has proved that an adult has salvaged but a small per cent of the vigor and instinctive guidance that were his in his childhood. We learn to live with ease only as we recontact the strength that once was ours. "Genius," wrote Coleridge, "is the power of carrying the feelings of childhood into the powers of manhood." To this the words of Lowell may well be added: "It is the privilege of genius that to it life never grows commonplace as to the rest of us."

It need not grow commonplace even when we are fourscore and ten, and he who refuses to let it do so by his very refusal finds within himself a genius he did not know was his. It is not his if he claims it as his own. It comes to him if he has reverence, gratitude and even worship for its flow.

Few men have had more deep regard for this divine spark than Washington Irving. "It is interesting," he said, "to note how some minds seem almost to create themselves, springing up under every disadvantage and working their solitary but irresistible way through thousands of obstacles." The little word "seem" is the key to this great sentence, for as the power comes to us and through us it *seems* most often to be *of* us. But do not the pictures and the words that pour from a television set seem to you to be made entirely by the instrument? Even a television set, like the human mind, must have many parts, and have them in order, for it to receive any and all

235

programs. While it does not create them, it must be correctly constituted to reproduce them. So too with human personality. "Men of genius do not excel in any profession because they labor in it," wrote Hazlitt, "but they labor because they excel."

Our varying gifts then play a vital part, not only in how well we receive the guiding programs by which we wisely live, but as to what those programs are. To believe as genius does in our power to receive is also essential to the development of the capacity. Without this guidance our wisdom is insufficient to deal with the problems of so tumultuous a world. Speaking of this need, Samuel Johnson wrote that the divine flame is "that quality without which judgment is cold and knowledge inert: that energy which collects, combines, amplifies and animates."

If all men have within them some measure of such a power, why have they not used it constantly? Why has a gift we had as a child been so disrespected? The answer is not far to seek. Mankind as an inert mass reveres the commonplace, fearing what is not physically obvious and blatantly ordinary. "There is a sacred horror of anything grand," wrote Victor Hugo.

Hatred of the unusual is soon produced in a child whose parents deprive him of his creative power. He does not know what it is that he has lost, but senses that it was something that lifted him above the humdrum level. If he cannot keep it as his own, then no one else shall possess it. "When a true genius appears in the world," wrote Swift, "you may know him by this sign: that the dunces are all in confederation against him." This is not quite true. It is not the dunces who disparage the divine flame, but those who are sure that they themselves are smart. Goethe put his finger on this significant fact when he said: "Fools and sensible men are equally innocuous. It is in the half fools and the half wise that the danger lies."

Oxenham furthered this idea by putting it in verse:

> The high soul climbs the high way,
> The low soul gropes the low;
> And in between in the misty flats
> The rest drift to and fro.

Lastly, we might take to our hearts an admonishment from Sir Philip Sidney: "A dull head thinks of no better way to show himself wise than to suspect everything in his way."

It is not only the dull heads, however, who have been guilty of this crude skepticism, but those as well whom the world deems erudite. Many are the sophisticates with professional pomp whose myopia is such that everything they consider to be spiritual is relegated to the ashcan.

The average man gives no such violent response, but at the same time if you talk to him about a dynamic center of energy within himself he at once assumes that you are preaching at him. He resists you because he thinks you are being mystical. This illusion is caused by the fact that you are speaking to him about something with which he has become unfamiliar, and which therefore seems to him to be removed from the mundane world. It has to do with the invisible plane of life, and thus to him an unprovable area of existence.

Just so primitive man must have viewed every advancement toward what we now call civilization. For centuries he had had only his brawn to depend upon, and he expected no other way of life. When he saw the first wheel in motion he thought its power was made possible by the magic of a demon god. He had no awarenesses beyond the use of his own body. Few still have any thought or feeling beyond the toil of their own intellects. Identified now with their minds rather than their bodies, their self-awareness is, as we have shown, as limited to self-propelling as was that of ancient man to his bodily effort.

In contrast to the way millions of those whose experience limits them to the confines of their egos, the great men of modern science—such thinkers as Eddington and Jeans—have now no such constricted attitude. Speak to them of a center of power in man, and you are greeted at once by an open and comprehending response. They know that, however we may appear to be creatures of muscle and bone, every one of our physical manifestations is composed of colonies of cells, each an electromagnetic charge. They know that just as you can from ignorance fail wisely to use the instruments of science and mechanics, so you can fail in the harnessing of your dynamic strength.

While the average man will not give you this intelligent comprehension of a center of power, he may unknowingly exhibit its vigor when some sudden situation comes upon him. Impelled by rage or fear, men have performed amazing feats, and even sex and wonder have released energies that rival those of Hercules. Not even a tiger dares to confront a mother wolf bent on the protection of her young. Such are her reserves of courage, released by her maternal urge, that few of the great cats could survive her onslaught. Everywhere in the world are evidences of a cosmic surge in living organisms that rivals the endurance and force of atomic energy. Just as many minerals were long neglected, so have the sources of man's majestic vigor been hidden and ignored.

It is a noteworthy fact—reported again and again by careful observers—that in times of crisis apparently ordinary people show great courage. In a shipwreck or after the ravages of a tornado an almost unbelievable strength of spirit seems to appear in those who in their usual life revealed no such poise. Most evidently there is potential heroism in most of us, a soul vigor that we neglect to use in our daily experiences.

Have there not been times in your own life when you did something with ease and without self-consciousness as if some force that seemed to come from beyond yourself was operative? Have you not at such a time been lifted up as if you had drunk an elixir that gave you the strength of ten, and an inspiration that was kindred to the wisdom of genius? Would not your life lose much of its strain if you took time to contact this psychic geyser?

Many of man's buoyant capacities have, incongruously enough, heavy names; none more so than the electromagnetic energy that motivates his being. It is called dynamogeny. It means that you have a central power station much like that possessed by TVA or any system, public or private, that generates the current that lights your home. It reaches to every part of your organism even as the power systems now cover our land.

While these man-made instruments are new, the principles that made them possible are ancient and cosmic. Our human achievements are but part of the dynamics of nature. Nor is there, as modern science has proved, a living organism, even down to the amoeba, that is not electromagnetic in nature. It would otherwise have no vitality.

Few have realized that in living creatures this power is of a spiritual nature, and that it has been moving before man's eyes for centuries yet almost completely ignored by the multitude.

To free ourselves of debatable terminology as to this psychic energy, we might well use the simple Finnish term *sisu*. In that far northern clime, *sisu* is the word used by everyone to designate inner power. It is not left to the mercies of philosophical erudition. Lin Root, in an article in the June, 1955, *Reader's Digest*, wrote: "The qualities here embodied: integrity, endurance, determination, courage, independence, deep feeling for nature and art, exist in varying degrees in every Finn. . . . They are the building blocks of the Finnish character, which is expressed in their word *sisu*."

One could hardly find a better definition of the dynamic center of spiritual strength or of a quality more needed by the citizens of present-day America.

Pause for a little while to consider how different your life might have been had your parents, as soon as you could talk, taught you to seek, to listen for and to depend upon the intuitive power of your *sisu*. You are familiar with the description of the wisdom and achievement of the disciples after the Holy Ghost had come into them, as Jesus had promised it would. But have you ever, as the Finnish people have, had the habit of turning to this dynamic center of your being? Perhaps you have, as a religious concept, and while using prayer. But has it been a guide to energize and promulgate all you do? Do you now, at this moment, so fully believe in the strength, wisdom and courage of this hero in your heart that you let it be your guide and source of vigor in all your life? Do you use the intuition it endows as would some boy or girl in Finland whose parents had taught their children this secret for the conquest of fate?

That is a pregnant question, for upon it depends one's ability to use all the great therapies successfully, and not in the halfhearted, mechanical manner with which the average person strives to apply them.

After more than half a century spent in psychological work, let me say that any and all of the great means of easing out of strain—image-making, autosuggestion and the actuation process—can fail you, and fail you utterly, if you attempt to use them in the way you might depend upon the many mechanical gadgets in your home. One needs to give to each of these great methods a spiritual co-operation and the cosmic energy that comes from his *sisu*.

Unlike the Finnish peasants, most of us have known no such word as *sisu*. He who in a spirit of gratitude and of reverence reaches deeply back into himself for his *sisu* to act as his guide and giver of courage, lives with invincible strength even when confronted with herculean obstacles. He may call it an odic force, mana, prana, a divine influx, that he depends upon. His faith may name it the Holy Ghost, or with modern men of science he may define it as a dynamogeny made possible by the reception of the cosmic rays, it does not matter. There are even agnostics who believe in the reception of a radiant energy by all that lives.

It makes no difference what terms we use; we shall become lost indeed if we spend our attention on the variations of words. The important thing is to believe, as a little Finnish child would do, in the presence and power of the *sisu* and then to use it as our center of strength in all we do.

When a whole people has demonstrated the presence of a dynamic power within mankind, need we resort to psychological tests before we have faith in what it can accomplish for us? May we not rightly become somewhat skeptical of laboratory proof that sets limitations, denying that such gifts exist? Are not the evidences greater when they are demonstrated in life? The so-called scientific testing is usually done in an artificial setting which one might suppose would invalidate any restrictive conclusions.

Some time ago a well-known experimenter decided to determine the intelligence of cats. He tested *one* cat in a laboratory and stated that the I.Q. of the species is low. I will wager my whole reputation that if the same cat could have tested the psychologist out in the woods, she would have decided he was a moron. Having played with Indian boys in my childhood, I personally belong to forest and stream; their lore is second nature for me. I know that that psychologist could not have done as well in the big woods as a feeble-minded boy of my acquaintance.

When it comes, therefore, to forces within us of a subjective and extrasensory nature, objectively achieved conclusions as to their existence are ridiculous. I emphasize this point because I would have you believe in the invisible power of heroism, even if there are those all about you who would deny them because they do not respond to laboratory analysis. The testimony of a nation is a better proof than we shall ever get from the investigations of those who require and never achieve a material demonstration of spiritual realities.

Nor is this modern manifestation by Finland of true courage and inherent wisdom the only evidence of its existence. History has its use as a measurer of man and history reveals that since time was humanity has believed in and exhibited an almost divine oracle in the soul of man. Its dynamic strength has been called, as I have said, by various names: cosmic power, etheric vigor and radiant energy. Its source has been as variously named as radioactive rays, divine influx and the inflow of the Holy Ghost. Aristotle called the receiver of this power the hylearche. Others have used the term telarche, while to religious leaders it seemed synonymous with conscience.

Each time you depend upon your center of power, you deepen the channel through which it flows.

In other words, you establish a channel between all your mental attributes and the motive force that produces your will. This makes possible a form of automation in personality, and there is in human life no greater application of constructive design than such a therapeutic development. There is no procedure that so eases one out of strain as the flow such a process makes possible. By this therapeutic automation you connect your center of power, that is, the group of hopes, interests and loves that mean most to you, and connect them with the tasks you have to perform and the obstacles you need to conquer. The momentum of your desires and the strength of your enthusiasm then carry you to victory.

Many a battle has been won by this tide of purpose. During the Civil War, General Grant asked one of his aides by whose order a body of troops were storming a hill. "By their own, sir," came the answer of their captain, who had been unable to restrain the passion of his men. Nor are there many enemies who can withstand such a momentum as it rolls up and over the crest of a barricade.

So too with your life and mine. The passions within us, the hungers, longings, cravings and hopes are aspects of our center of power—interests, loves and enthusiasms—capable of becoming so associated with what we must do as to produce a drive that seems to accomplish our purposes for us. The desire "becomes happened." Great is the power of therapeutic automatism, greater still the inevitable energy of a full momentum.

No therapy is more important than to remind ourselves of this dynamic strength, and thus to learn to use it more constantly. A firm conviction that this reserve is there suffices to bring it into action in many lives.

After nearly half a century of clinical practice, during which time I have had to deal with every sort of human problem, I can say—and say it emphatically—that this center of courage and quiet strength is latent in everyone, and that a belief in this fact is an essential attribute of all helpful therapies.

To some people there is a religious aspect to this latent power. They find it best by the use of prayer. To others it appears to be what William James called "a second wind."

Several of the European psychiatrists speak of it as a reservoir of energy of a glandular nature. In any case, there is something in us majestic enough to be thought divine, real enough to be biological in origin, powerful enough to transform our relation to daily experience, and strangely capable of endowing a guidance as to what to do that is often extraordinary in its scope. Plato named it the energy of the soul, and spoke of it with almost the same reverence Jesus gave to the Holy Ghost. Philosophers of a later period dealt with it as "the capacity for inspiration," believing that when Jesus told his disciples they could be given the wisdom as to what to say and do, he had this form of inspiration in mind.

In any case, modern research has proved that such a courage is possible. It has also shown that an amazing physical endurance comes with it. In peace as well as war and under all sorts of hardship, not only an unbelievable strength, but an amazing wisdom has come to countless people, sustaining them through an ordeal by which they would otherwise have been overcome.

Many thereby have discovered this most important means of the conquest of fate: a belief in and constant dependence upon this spiritual center of being. They have discovered, moreover, that the more they turn to this potential heroism, the more wisely and vigorously it acts.

There is nothing sentimental about a belief in such a sustaining power or the intuition it endows. Even a potato knows how to grow after its kind and to sprout without needing to be told when to do it. Should we not emulate a potato, and believe we too possess innate wisdom and a center of strength capable of transforming our relation to life when and as we use it?

When sophisticated people fail successfully to apply the great therapies it is because they do not turn to this center of strength as an essential attribute of every constructive process. Simple-hearted men, on the other hand, have little difficulty with such methods. They wonder why anyone would think them difficult. Jed Murray used to run a black sloop in Casco Bay and cruise in it at times along the Maine coast seeking the elusive halibut. Fogs meant nothing to him. Even in the darkest night he always knew where he was.

On one occasion I tried, while in Jed's presence, to explain to my companion how one used an intuitive process and merged it with a timing sense to guide him in his feats of navigation. My listener, a college professor, found it hard to follow me while Jed had no trouble at all.

"Don't you see," he interrupted, "I don't do anything the other fellers don't do. Lots of 'em goes every morning out of their coves in a dory, rows ten miles up the coast in a thick fog pulling up their lobster pots all the way and then goes back into their little coves not wider'n a barnyard."

"That doesn't tell me how you or they do it," the learned professor objected.

"It's the same way a pig goes home, if he gets away from the feller you've sold him to," Jed explained.

"And the pig does it . . . how?" the professor pressed.

"I guess he jes' listens to the buzz of his wireless beam," Jed laughed. "There's a couple of martins been comin' to my barn fer years. Turn up each spring, prompt as can be. I don't know where they winter—somewhere in South America, I s'pose. Must take quite a bit of navigation to git here. I guess they have faith that some power will guide 'em if they'll let it."

"And you have that faith?" the professor asked softly, as if doing some thinking along new lines.

"That's it," Jed nodded. "Seems like, as Dave says, I have a sort of time sense. and a picturing power that works together.

I sort of see inside myself where I am and how to get to a place."

"I understand," the professor smiled. "I know something of the personal power of which you speak."

I wonder if he did.

There have of course always been men and women who, without knowing such terms as "*sisu*," "telarche" or "center of power," have felt an impelling depth in their beings, a dynamic strength that gave them guidance and courage. This must have been true in prehistoric days, long before any psychology or a philosophy of life was conceived or understood. You may have friends and associates who have never opened a book or ever come in contact with the idea of inner guidance and spiritual strength. You may have observed in them an imperturbable calm and a quiet fortitude. Be sure that, whether they know it or not, they were depending on a center of guidance and power within themselves.

You will find, moreover, that when you, too, form the habit of seeking this creative strength and deeply attend to its impelling, you will have conquered strain. Your way of life will be transformed.

Learning to turn to and to use your center of power, as the Finnish children are taught to do, is the twenty-third step in the great and simple art of letting nature pour her forces into and through you so as to empower all you do.

24 THE TECHNIQUE OF LINKAGE

O F ALL the gifts of man the free association process is the one which comes nearest to being an agent of the *sisu*. We have previously discussed its use, and spoken of it as the vehicle through which inspiration flows. We need at this point to remember that fact, and to relate it to the art of receiving guidance and power from our center of being. If such a remembering is done often enough, it establishes a connection between one's inner power and one's habits of thought. Free association thereby becomes an instrument of intuition and of spiritual insight. The fact that being an association process it is a coherently connected line of thought yet at the same time free—that is, uncontrolled by your ego —allows it to become controlled by the creative guidances.

There is, therefore, no more important aspect of the mind to understand than that of free association. It becomes an instrument by which each and all of the therapies we have discussed are empowered, since it is the means by which they are connected with the "sublime flame." It does not, however, act as a separated spark that motivates each technique, but rather of all of them together.

For this reason the greatest mental efficiency comes to pass when the therapies are linked together as a single procedure, and made to function as one instrument. Then by association this unit of accomplishment is again linked with the things we have to do and the problems we have to meet. An effortless and spontaneous achievement thereupon results. When, moreover, this mighty union of therapies is empowered by inspiration, intuition, instinctive guidance, intelligence—use what words you will—it develops into a majestic, psychic automation, a means that once and for all establishes the ways to good living.

Let us realize at this point that the gaining of this great power need not be a difficult or complicated process. Nor must you know and understand everything about it all at once. All you have to do, in fact, is to become interested in the use of free association. If you are willing to experiment with it and give yourself time, all the rest that pertains to effortless thought and spontaneous accomplishment will result of its own accord. *Letting* things constructively develop is the very soul and sinew of the new way of living.

It would be foolish indeed to slave and to coerce oneself into effortless achievement when coercion is the very evil that deprived one of personal automation in the first place. Nor could we expect to learn how to release our inherent guidance and constructively to use intuition and inspiration by applying the processes of strain that have denied to us these natural procedures.

Just in itself, moreover, there is no mental gift more wonderful than the intuition that the free association process makes possible, if you allow it to act for you without self-conscious interference. Let the stream flow. Be grateful that you have it. Listen to its voice as you would to the words of a great speaker. All sorts of information, and a wisdom you did not know was available to you, will then move along the association stream.

It is better not to remember than to become tense from trying to do so. Give up the overeffort, and the facts and figures you want will appear for you of their own free will.

It has been stated that linkage is the most important of all the psychotherapies. While it is simple in itself, it needs careful study. It consists in connecting your desires with your will, or center of power, so that the energy of that center is constructively used to accomplish the acts you wish to fulfill. Every designer in the field of engineering uses linkage. He may not know the process by name, but it would never occur to him to ignore it in his objective operations. But almost everyone else, and even a well-educated engineer, ignores it in the subjective operations of his personality. To this strange neglect we owe some of the failure in life, all the suicides, more than half of the physical diseases and much of the flood of psychoneurosis and insanity that is filling our hospitals. An extreme statement, you say? Wait until you have read all of the facts.

You will admit, will you not, that the failure of one's desires for achievement, comfort and affluence in the material world, and of love, companionship and permanence in the sphere of human relations, is a major aspect in our distress, unhappiness and ill health? To be able to fulfill one's normal hopes for personal expansion and abundant love would remove from individual experience most of its disappointments and strains.

You will also admit, will you not, that to succeed in each of these fields of longing requires some energy, a wise use of your strengths and a thoughtful avoidance of your weaknesses? You do not win a place in the world by ignoring the making of sensory equivalents, or by allowing your self-indulgences and immaturities to control your conduct. You succeed only by the use of your ability to work with concentration and attention, even when you use visual imagery and all the other therapies.

Let us get down to the practical point then, which is this: that every designer and operator in the sphere of engineering uses, as we have already said, the law of connections of contiguity, and depends on it to harness and develop power. But almost no one understands and intelligently uses this essential method to develop and use power in his own life. He makes a haphazard application of it, but seldom a comprehensive and efficient one.

For centuries man used windmills to pump water, grind grain and accomplish many activities that were beyond his patience or his strength. Can you imagine that even a moron in antiquity would have expected a windmill to work with no wind to move the great fans? And would the windmill have been of any use if it had not been so connected as to transmit the power to a pump or to some other mechanism?

Before man sailed a boat he paddled with oars. Without this means of propelling the craft it did not move in accordance with his desire. At one time oxen were harnessed to a turnstile or horses put in a treadmill to accomplish work. Whatever the source of energy, it had to be linked to the instrument that was to do the work or nothing was accomplished. A chain, a belt or a shaft became necessary to convey the source of strength to the purposive mechanism.

Nor has this principle even been abandoned, and never can it be. Can you conceive that in the most backwoods of lumber mills anyone would try to make a power saw act without an engine, or expect the engine to work without steam from a boiler, gasoline from a tank or in place of it an electrical connection to a motor? The lights in your house may come from a whirling dynamo, but it does not whirl of its own accord unless the rushing power of a river is fed into a water turbine, or the steam from boilers is piped into an engine which then uses that invisible vapor.

Association linkage is also the process by which such connections are established when used in the field of human conduct. It consists in stopping, as everyone does who operates a machine, quietly to turn on the right amount of power, and to see that that power is properly transmitted to the productive instrument. There must be the sensory equivalents of a belt, a chain or a shaft, pipes with valves or electric lines with switches in our setup just as in each and every mechanical process. These must be opened by a thoughtful and deliberate act.

That such an act is needed in human engineering is most obvious. It is also not hard to accomplish because, if you will let it, it will accomplish itself by means of association linkage, a process easily made from a repetitive application of visual imagery, autosuggestion and actuation.

We should stop, however, when the linkage has become established, to see that it is connected with our ruling hopes, interests and loves, and that by the use of visualization, autosuggestion and actuation it is connected with what we wish to do. We then thereby knowingly and purposively open the valve so that our individual generator comes successfully into play.

Linkage has a thousand uses and meets innumerable needs. By its considered application almost any reasonable desire can be fulfilled and nearly every obstacle overcome. Intellectual automation is an inevitable result.

Instead of using this practical means, millions of people still accept the wearisome mental routines directed by their surface intellects. With most of their valves closed, their belts loose, their shafts needing lubricant and the electric currents all but shut off, they strive in a mood of nervous egotism as if they must use their psychic brawn in all accomplishment.

Never was there a greater madness. Even a savage knows enough to use a lever to move a stone. He does not bend his back clawing at the rock with his two hands. Many a banker, in contrast, tries to lift the dead weight of his financial problems as if he of himself could do it. He acts as if no instruments were available to ease his tasks. When in middle life he dies of heart failure, the obituary speaks of his great loyalty to his responsibilities. It is to the asininities of egotism he has been loyal, and thus he has ignored the means that modern intelligence should use, instead of the prideful "himselfness" he abuses.

Let us repeat and never forget that we are at the high pitch of a great mechanical age, but entering a psychological era. That it will be quite as significant and as startlingly full of miracles as that of any period in man's history is now evident. No single factor in the coming of this era of personality efficiency is more significant, or will it do more to bring the new era to pass, than the realization that every process in physics, chemistry, engineering and in all the objective sciences has *its psychical or subjective counterpart* in the operation of the human mind.

This discovery is as important to mankind as knowledge of navigation or that the earth is round, for it opens up vast prospects of personal power, of unusual accomplishments and magnificent ease for the fulfillments of the human being. Every gadget that facilitates housework for a woman, every process appearing in this atomic age of radio and radar *has its human equivalent.* Some day what we call extrasensory perception and psychic phenomena will not seem paranormal.

Man will then know that the supernatural is only the natural that is not yet understood. He will also know that there is no end to the manifestation of personal power that association linkage makes possible. It makes it possible for him to originate and to design even as nature does. It empowers him so that, as Emerson put it, he becomes part of the cosmic force as a maker of the useful, the beautiful and true. It is also the gift that penetrates below the surface of life to understand the meaning behind form. One then perceives the purposes beneath action, the motives that generate substance. One comprehends at long last the connotations in the denotations, the implications beyond the explicit facts. Without this extrasensory capacity, man would have had no grasp of the noumena that design all phenomena and bring them into being.

Should we not have such awe when made aware of these great powers of automation that we free ourselves forever from egotism, and let these mighty attributes work *within* us and *for* us?

Various of the therapies are only useful at certain times. Cool intellectual reason may be important before you become engaged but dangerous afterward. Spontaneous enthusiasm is good when listening to your sweetheart's song. It is not safe in a marital argument. Association linkage has no such limitation. It can even help you while making love. In that most challenging human activity do you not need intuition, inspiration and courage? Does it not call for an abundant flow of magnetism to give you a winning charm? Is not a linkage with your *sisu* most important at such a pitch of high emotion?

It is in the series of little acts as much as in the fulfillment of the great purposes that this technique is essential. Can you imagine how sustained you would feel if you had a group of invisible wise men or a band of charm-producing houris always at your command to instruct you telepathically as to what to do and say, how to do and say it, to tell you why each situation is as it is, whom to depend upon and when to act? Would you not feel *rich* in power and security? And would you not then know that you could use your wisdom just where it was needed? That is the way this therapy makes one feel.

For the sake of emphasis, and because so few individuals actively use this essential means to good fortune, let me repeat that its power is obtained by uniting visual imagery, induced autosuggestion, the actuation process and association linkage into sensory equivalents as one interrelated procedure through which the inner power—*sisu*—can flow. Then a linkage may be formed between this union and one's center of power—*sisu* —and the whole creative procedure becomes one dynamic therapy. It acts as a single instrument even though composed of several parts, just as your motorcar is a single instrument despite the fact of its many elements.

At this point we should again emphasize that none of one's intellectual powers is ever discarded because of this automatic way of thinking. They are not given up or displaced. They are organized and used.

If you have not tried association linkage long enough for it to have become an unconscious strength, acting for you spontaneously when problems press, then you need to apply this method consciously and painstakingly at whatever time the conditions are most difficult. Dear old Dr. Ross in the Design Course at Harvard used to say, "We work for order, and hope for beauty." In adjustment psychology we consciously apply this great therapy, and hope that spontaneous automation will result. At Harvard, we students of design discovered that if we strove hard to master the principles, after awhile these cosmic laws seemed to "get into our blood," and we obeyed them without thought when at work on any aesthetic task. This "into one's blood" is the way the great therapy should work when situations call for its action.

Such a method is not a philosophy, and should not be forced to substitute for one. Philosophies are guidances as to the general aspects of experience. Therapies are methods for dealing with particular tasks and problems. One applies the great therapy therefore where changes, adjustments, transitions and transmutations need to take place.

For further emphasis let me state that in its deepest form linkage is the act of associating in your mind the passion of some love, the urge of some hope or the impelling of some interest—or all of them together—for the achieving of a task you need to accomplish or the conquest of some difficulty you are striving to overcome. It is as if you then tap hereditary guidances that have directed the ways of all living organisms since time was. Even a mastodon had to have instincts to tell him how and what to eat. Nor is there a gadfly without an innate sense as to the best way to fulfill its personality.

The technique of linkage is, as it were, a means of establishing an unconscious reminder to call upon all the instinctive guidances, intelligent endowments and will power a man has so that these forces come into play of their own accord. They do not do so repetitively until their organized presence becomes a habit deeply established. Then it is as if some mighty force moved through the self, achieving the tasks it has to do, quietly and efficiently. What was toil heretofore becomes a creative accomplishment. Trouble instead of being something to dread is turned into an object for adventure.

We live on the basis of quickened energy. Everything that takes place outside of us is an urging which creates within us an impulse to act according to our basic natures, our state of maturity, our education and preparation for life. If our state of being is psychoneurotic because of abnormal conditioning, we give back an unnatural response to the stimulus. If it is an ignorant state, we give back ignorance and unpreparedness. If, on the other hand, we have been taught to understand our minds and have learned to apply their capacities in the handling of experience, after they became habits, they function as automatic responses to the stimulus of events.

No one, in so complex a world as ours, can successfully "use his head" all the time. If he must always "think what to do" and constantly decide on each course of action, he will soon wear out from the strain of overworked attention. We should not have to live by continued self-concern. We can and should be carried by emotions flowing in constructive habits of thought and action.

Musso has proved with little galvanometers that when emotion flows into your thought, your action or your thinking is done without any wear and tear on the cells. But what you do without that emotional drive produces tremendous nerve and cell exhaustion. That is being proved all over the world today in laboratories of various universities.

I like to repeat the story Dr. William MacDougall used to tell about a farmer who was chased by his wife with an ax in her hand after they had been married for twenty-nine years. He ran. He climbed up the rain conductor and along the edge of the roof. When he came out of his panic of fear he was sitting on the top of the chimney. He could not have done that even to save his life in his ordinary state of mind. The emotional drive set his organism going, and going well.

Those who have learned to use the association process as the means that will link together not only the therapies we have been discussing, but as a center of power to give those therapies dynamic energy, come almost to worship this mighty means of living. Consider, for instance, the transformation that takes place within one who for years may have had to push and strive, as if only by a stressful use of his own body and a straining of his mind he could deal with the problems of his days.

Let us conceive that such a man by the use of the association process learned how to create an automatic use of visual imagery, of autosuggestion and all the other therapies, as well as to release the dynamic from his center of power. What a magnificent transformation then takes place in his life. He no longer needs to strain as a personality. He has at his command powers equal to those that modern science and engineering have created in their transformation of the material world. His relation to his day and age is balanced at last.

You will find that if, or when, you become convinced of the practical use of linkage, a mighty change in your way of life has taken place. But it is only from a depth of conviction and a repetitive effort to establish linkage that it becomes permanently founded as the means by which you achieve your purposes. When you find tension or strain is developing, stop and remind yourself that there *is* a dynamic center within you and practical techniques which it can empower. Let the linkage process work for you. Don't do things of yourself. Turn to this inner power and depend upon this human engineering within you.

Every time you do this, instead of letting your ego coerce you and drive your nerves into a tense condition, endeavor to strengthen the habit of automatic activity, the habit of using an organized state of being with its inherent abilities. Even as the bird flies effortlessly, the fish swims from natural guidance, so you will live and achieve as easily and guidedly as all the other living things that find and use the wisdom nature has stored within them.

Learning through the use of the association process to link one's latent strength with every technique and therapy, so that they merge and are used as one great and single means of poise and power in every process of living, is the twenty-fourth and final step in the art of living without tension.

25 DYNAMIC PRACTICALITY

*W*HEN great epochs come to pass few people realize that anything unusual is taking place. They go about their drab routine as if nothing were happening. Many, however, realize that we are today faced with a major crisis: the ever encroaching threat of another war. Only a few see that this impending danger is playing a vital part in one of the greatest transitions in history—the awakening of millions to the power of man's mind.

Nor is this all. A new faith in spiritual values is giving a deeper meaning to life. It is bringing an awareness which will do much, even most, to end war and its causes forever. It will also change our personal relation to destiny.

Threatened by an untrustworthy enemy, every nation needs a strong defense. Behind our arms, however, moral and spiritual courage is essential. Had we remained absorbed in the materialism of past decades, America might have been overcome by enemy power; not by bombs alone, but by a supine indifference and a somnolent selfishness.

It is doubtful if such a disaster can now come to pass. As individuals, as a nation and even as a continent, we are awakening to the importance of life's deeper realities. We are taking our place as men and women capable of loving God and the neighbor, holding at long last to an enduring faith.

Today science no longer contends these spiritual values. A new sense of brotherhood is also stirring in the mind of industry. Education is turning from its adherence to scientific factualism toward a belief in creative processes. This concludes centuries of conflict. We are, in consequence, possessors of a new strength.

This is the change that is taking place, and in the coming of this epoch the new attitude of science plays a major part. Many of its leaders now accept the powers of an invisible universe, and the actuality of the soul. Some believe they have proved the existence of the soul, and of a creative guidance as well, a veritable Holy Ghost, speaking to the minds of men and leading them forward with divine understanding. Nor is this a mere opinion, but the thoughtful conclusion from laboratory tests, telescopic research and statistical compilation.

Religion took the presence of the soul on faith, which was well, for had it not held grimly to its belief through the age of materialism, mankind would have sunk to the brute. Instead of contending this passion of faith, science now fortifies it by experiment and mathematical exactitude. Science does not ask us to believe on faith alone, nor does it coerce us to discard our doubts. It quietly presents to us its documented evidence. That brings a new epoch indeed.

Proof of the existence of the soul will in time change the relation to life of every man, woman and child. It will regenerate religion, reanimate philosophy, vitalize psychology, rejuvenate education and open the heart of commerce, industry and labor to the way "on earth as it is in heaven."

There isn't an ounce of sense in living anything but a riotous life, unless we are more than bones.

The time comes to every man when he must take counsel with himself and ask what he is and why he is concerned with any life beyond food, frivolity and fornication. Actually, to sit on a palm-fringed beach while sun-kissed maidens frolic adoringly is far more comfortable than following the North Star.

There is no reason for personal effort unless the soul is, and unless it is immortal. To strive to enrich your consciousness and then to have it become dust and ashes would be ridiculous. To love and then to suffer anguish, thinking death had taken the loved one forever, would be madness. Better to indulge in revelry and song if this is all there is to it.

Since, however, the efforts we make are evidences of a something within us that is more than flesh, it is important to realize how this inner being functions. When, as in prayer, we create dynamic images of our spiritual intent, we turn our forces concordantly in one direction. It is a unity of action not unlike the magnetizing of steel, whose elements are thereby impelled in one direction. As a result, we open ourselves to the inflowing of etheric energy, thereby becoming recipients of more abundant life. We enter into harmony with the dynamic flow of creation, passing out of chaos into cosmic calm.

Such a conception as this would have seemed mystical a hundred years ago. Today it appears so only to mundane minds. Insight into the mysteries of matter has changed our understanding of spirit.

Every man knows he is more than a mountain of muscle. He senses the presence of his invisible nature. He feels the majesty of his mind. He knows, too, that only by constructive effort, enduringly maintained, is his life flung forward; only as he determines upon an upward climb is it ever made.

Such a seeking for spiritual growth comes from no mere moral choice, no superficial obedience to ethical standards nicely adapted to the social shibboleths. Here is a cosmic process releasing the dynamics of one's being. Nor is the power that brings this evolution to pass a physical energy. Something creative and celestial is taking place. Life is manifesting its divinity.

That your soul will live eternally, none who senses the miracle of personality can ever doubt. Something *is* when a human being comes into existence.

This means, of course, that a new vision must motivate all we do, from the making and using of our gadgets, to our revaluing and understanding of mechanics and science. Our achievement in the mastery of matter must be vitalized by our awareness of and manifestation of the soul.

It also means that we must learn to live by inspiration: a guidance that is not mystical but in all aspects practical. We shall then not only have found our own souls, but learned to live from the power and guidance they receive.

The term personal power is itself a paradox, for power is not personal in the sense that it is self-generated. A human being might well be typified by an electric motor. He receives the power that appears to be himself through the instruments of his nature that also seem to be his. We speak of a man's hands or a man's head, but it is natural for all mankind to have hands and heads. Power is an element of life, and life as radiant energy flows into every vital being. Power is the result of etheric or electromagnetic influx.

To believe with men of modern science that we receive our power from cosmic and radioactive rays is most important, for the more one identifies himself with the reception of power the more one receives it. It flows into him as he uses it. In the last analysis, it flows through him.

Unless we let this power motivate us, that is, unless we use it and depend upon it, it cannot flow through us, and hence does not, to the same degree, come into us. Viewed from the attitude of modern astrophysics, there is nothing mysterious, mystic, esoteric or occult about this reception of energy.

Historians have long pointed out that events create great men. Washington, they tell us, would have been a mediocre planter but for the American Revolution. The need to possess and to use heroic energy opens the way for it to flow into and through a man.

Those who have the attitude of bravery and seek a great purpose become like fine machines that need and call for extra power. This development may happen to anyone who constructively desires it. Men remain mediocre only when they select mediocrity. How is it that the Finnish *sisu* is not the possession of just a few people in that northern clime, but the attribute of a nation? It is because each little child is taught to want it, that he can have it and that he will need it. This he believes. The belief opens him to its reception.

The more stress there is in your life, the more power you can possess, *if* you want it. It is the stress that Finland has experienced that caused her people to ask for the power that has come into them as persons. He who would be a hero becomes a hero if he thinks and lives heroically.

When your troubles are great, therefore, do not become faint-hearted and depressed. Ask for the power needed for your task. Do not try to do things of yourself as an arrogant ego, and thus become blocked by strain. Believe that an influx of energy and guiding inspiration can be yours, and you too will have a *sisu*.

Let us not waste our breath debating the idle issue as to whether we have in our hearts some of the passion that empowered the knights of old. Let us dare to believe the flame is not lost. Victor Hugo, seeing the lassitude about him, feared heroes could no longer be. His dread was unfounded. There is a Hercules in every man, albeit he is often asleep. It is now that he must awake.

In a little book titled *On Vital Reserves*, William James wrote two great essays: "Hidden Energies of Men" and "The Gospel of Relaxation." He taught us that tension and strain shut off power and that the relaxation that comes from faith in the influx of radiant energy opens one up to its reception. He also made clear that this power may seem to fail us even as when a runner gasps for breath, but that if we keep on and have faith in it, the strength will return, even as a second wind comes to a determined athlete. Power is found where it is needed, if we keep on doing our work as if we were invincible. By so doing we so become.

It is pitiful, however, that so few people in the world at large have learned to relax and to let this sublime energy serve them. It is tragic that, instead of a calm turning of thought and feeling inward, seeking to contact this divine flow, almost everyone, and especially those in trouble, focus frantically on the situations outside of them, as if they alone by their wits and brawn could cope with their dilemmas.

You need not any longer toil as if only your ego with its muscle can do your work, or push your difficulties aside. Such a way of life belongs to the time when fagots and candles lighted our houses, when a wood fire gave the only heat, when water had to be lifted from a well by the pull and push of hands, when man had no means beyond himself to do his work. We know that below the surface layer of superstition and prejudice, there has been in each man a potential system not so different from a great generating plant with its spans of wires spread out in every direction to be used in the accomplishment of our innumerable tasks. Not knowing that this central plant is there, millions have failed to use it and ended their days in exhaustion, failure and disease.

Consider the case of a man who has lost contact with his inner guidance and is in some financial worry. Where is the focus of his attention? Is it not on whether or not he is going to get a certain amount of money? Is he not concerned as to whether some deal he is working on will come through, or how his partner is going to behave? Is not his thought fixed on what the men in his company are doing or whether the stock market is going up or going down? His focus of attention is on what he calls the practical, which, without inner guidance, is the impractical.

This is true because they who put their whole focus of attention outside themselves, setting it anxiously on the external problems, do not understand a primary principle: that all life functions by the action of a stimulus-response bond. It is an inner stimulus you need. What takes place inside of you decides whether you have any chance to change circumstances. It is the guidance from your soul that clarifies the decision. In other words, practicality consists not only in knowing how to use forethought, reason and memory, but in empowering those mental processes with instinctive guidance and divine inspiration.

Let us consider the anxiety of a woman in a marriage problem who has lost her faith in love. What is she doing? Is she not brooding over the way her husband is behaving without seeking the help of her *sisu*? Is she not emotionally involved in what may happen to her home? Pride makes her shrink from the idea that anyone should know there is any difficulty in relation to her husband. She is full of rage at the way her husband is behaving, without any regard to the way she herself may be causing it. The impersonal insight of her *sisu* might open her eyes. Instead she has a desperate dread as to the outcome. Her whole being is fixed on the possible consequences. She thinks that is being practical. She is being most impractical, for she has forsaken quiet meditation within her own mind by which alone a solution may be achieved.

Every difficuly in life is part of our spiritual development. Each is an experience through which, and by which, we grow. If we quietly accept each situation, whatever it may be, as an opportunity within ourselves, constructively to seek the guidance of our inner flame and use it to deal with problems in a positive manner, the best results that can be achieved in any given situation will come to pass.

When we become lost in egotistical anxiety, our attitude of self-concern destroys our spiritual receptivity. One then insists on doing everything of himself instead of its being done *through* him.

Arrogance and pride, jealousy and envy, competition and all the pressure of the mistaken attitudes of egotism, interfere with thinking and produce what we call closure. Closure is present when we become so involved in the situation that we cannot constructively receive guidance as to what to do. You have perhaps gotten into some difficulty with another person —a love conflict, a marriage problem, a partnership argument, a financial worry—and you found you couldn't think. You had closure. You were so emotionally worked up it shut off the inflow of spiritual power.

Guidance, inspiration, true thoughtfulness come when we reach for the voice of what is called the supraconscious and allow that voice, which comes from the kingdom of heaven within, to rise up and function through memory, reason, judgment and imagination. Only when we quietly turn back to that inner guidance, reach for it gently, relax to it, listen for it, can we fully function constructively.

You can make that change at any moment in your life if you wish to do so. That is the miracle. You can stop and say, "Get thee behind me Satan!" to all egotistical strain. You can affirm, "I'm going to turn to the constructive guidance within me and live that way no matter what the problem may be." Every time you fail to listen to the inner voice, remind yourself and go back to it again.

I personally believe that anything we do that is not built on that foundation is destined to some measure of failure, and everything we do that is built on that spiritual focus will inevitably, in some measure, succeed. The more we live in this way, the more we fulfill our life purposes. The more we stay with it, the greater our power and the surer our judgment.

This means that we can, if we will, increase our spiritual guidance and apply it to external experience. It means that we can make our adjustments in the realm of Caesar from a guidance that comes from God. We cannot deny that problems exist in everyday life. We cannot deny the decisions and applications that must be made. There are complexities to be dealt with. If we forsake the guidance from God, however, and only render unto Caesar, our lives go to pieces. Millions have been afraid to render unto God, and so have not known how to render unto Caesar. It is because of this loss of insight that we live in such an upset world.

Each time you turn to your center of power, it starts the forming of a habit path, and each time it is easier to do it again.

Habit is a mighty structure. A realization of this fact can give you a confidence in forces and factors of life beyond yourself yet in and of yourself. A new hope is born when you learn to make use of and to depend upon spiritual habit ways and see the ease they make possible.

Habit is not a principle that is only manifest in the life of man. Its nature is cosmic. It is the habit of the sun to rise at a certain moment each day. It is the habit of the moon to wax and wane. Modern science is a study of the habit ways of the cosmos. The attitude of the chemist and physicist is not essentially different from that of the astronomer. The habits of the stars are kindred to the habits of the electrons, the protons and all the other whirling attributes of the atom. As is the macrocosm, so is the microcosm. As is the structure of humanity, so is that of your being.

This insight into the self, as having powers within that are yet from forces beyond the self, is the center and sinew of our modern understanding. From it and upon it a new sense of being comes into life that can, if we let it, give to each of us a deeper courage and a truer calm.

That we may never forget, let us affirm, and again affirm, that it is the soul that knows. It alone is able to receive guidance and pass it on to consciousness. It alone has the power to merge the dynamic techniques and methods into one great, yet simple, therapy. It is the soul that in uniting the gifts of the mind empowers it with spontaneous energy. From a belief in this inspirational prescience one's thought turns away from adventitious compromise toward an obedient acceptance of the soul's gracious dominion. If one so lives, he lives with beauty and with ease. Then is a man a man, whose accomplishments give joy.

When an individual comes to this awareness and accepts his life adventure, he achieves insight into the deeper aspects of human consciousness and the wonders of the mind. He becomes an instrument of the universe, which is a synonym for being a child of nature. He cannot then feel insecure.

Petty values fall away. Anxiety has no place in such an attitude. The conquest of environment has taken place.

Let us affirm then that you and I have heroism in our depths, that there is a sleeping genius even in the most commonplace of individuals. The solution of insecurity and the command of circumstances lies in finding this inner courage and tapping the deep center of strength that is present within us. No one lives life well who does not live it daringly.

He alone uses the grandeur of the mind who believes in its grandeur. He is then able to permeate a small action with an atmosphere of greatness. With God all things are possible, and he who is with God becomes invincible. So it is that the dread of insecurity passes as we become secure within ourselves. Our right of choice again comes into action, and by its power our relation to every other person is transformed. We become human. We also become free.

FOREWORD TO THE SUBJECT INDEX

A table of contents can give you only a list of the chapters and a suggestion of a book's thought. A subject index, on the other hand, such as the one in the appendix of this book, serves a different and much-needed purpose. By means of its method of singling out the main ideas of the book and carrying each one through the complete volume, you have what is equivalent to a whole series of books. This is made possible by the rearrangement of the context.

Let us suppose that Mr. and Mrs. John Doe have this book in their home. Mr. Doe is interested in the question of business success and the development of useful social contacts. He will discover that by using the subject index this is a handbook on efficiency in the human-relational side of industry. Mrs. Doe, however, is not in the least concerned with business methods. She has four children, ages nineteen, sixteen, twelve and nine. The problems of her young, how to meet their needs, how to help in their education, what to do about her oldest girl's hypersensitive shyness, are all important to Mrs. Doe. She will find that by using the subject index, the book becomes a special treatise on the mental development and health of her children.

Let us suppose that Mary Doe, John's unmarried sister, lives with them. Being much younger than her brother, she is still of marrying age. But love has not come her way. Her heart is full of unsatisfied desire. There is much in the subject index about love and marriage, how to secure affection as well as how to keep it. As she applies this index, Mary Doe is impelled to use her imagination in a practical way. Her hope becomes stronger as she comes to understand that marriage doesn't hunt one out. Let us wish that she will take a job and day-times be out of the home. She would then meet eligible men. It won't be long after that before Mary marries.

Since no heavy technical terms are involved, even Charlie Doe may be seen from time to time reading the subject index. He is interested in ways to study more successfully, and there is something about the what-how-why-who-where-when method of thinking this book contains that fascinates any thoughtful boy. He will find that when he uses it in his school work he gets higher grades. It once lifted twelve of the lowest boys in a school of over five hundred to the honor list. Charlie will find that the subject index points out the relation of this process to education, and will discover he can gain personal benefit from thoughtful reading.

Maybe even Polly Doe will be seen thumbing over the subject index in that casual "of course, I'm not interested" manner of an adolescent. Maybe there will be pencil marks against the section on love. Perhaps the experience of be-coming a woman puzzles Polly. That, however, is a secret she won't talk about to anyone who is not her own age, but don't suppose she is reticent when in her group.

To expect Harry Doe, age nine, to read a book on human life is asking too much. Yet will he not watch his elders with that penetrating amusement that foreshadows an active inter-est in a few years? Maybe he will wonder if what they learn from their reading will give him a better break.

Let us suppose that you yourself are especially interested in the matter of health. You are often exhausted, and while not exactly sick are much below par. Turning to the subject index, you find the first reference on the top of page 12. It does not exactly deal with health. Why not? Because one first needs to achieve a new point of view toward the care of his body before specific methods of mental and physical hygiene can best be applied. For this reason, emphasis is placed in the first dozen or more references on the avoidance of strain. You will find, however, that it is not long before the subject index gives you much practical help that is specifically concerned with your mental and physical welfare.

272

Has not the subject index thereby served your special need? That it can do for all the designated problems. You will notice that such subjects as business psychology and the adjustments of home and children have many more references. This is because they are more pressing than some of the other subjects listed in the index.

SUBJECT INDEX*

* T—top of page; C—center of page; B—bottom of page.